THE FLIGHT OF PONY BAKER

A Boy's Town Story

W.D. HOWELLS

1st WORLD
LIBRARY
Literary Society

The Flight of Pony Baker

W. D. Howells

© 1st World Library, 2008
PO Box 2211
Fairfield, IA 52556
www.1stworldlibrary.com
First Edition

LCCN: 2007935417

Softcover ISBN: 978-1-4218-9367-9
Hardcover ISBN: 978-1-4218-9467-6
eBook ISBN: 978-1-4218-9267-2

Purchase *"The Flight of Pony Baker"*
as a traditional bound book at:
www.1stWorldLibrary.com/purchase.asp?ISBN=978-1-4218-9367-9

1st World Library is a literary, educational organization
dedicated to:

- Creating a free internet library of downloadable ebooks

- Hosting writing competitions and offering book publishing
scholarships.

Interested in more 1st World Library books? contact:
literacy@1stworldlibrary.com
Check us out at: www.1stworldlibrary.com

1st World Library Literary Society

Giving Back to the World

"If you want to work on the core problem, it's early school literacy."

- James Barksdale, former CEO of Netscape

"No skill is more crucial to the future of a child, or to a democratic and prosperous society, than literacy."

- Los Angeles Times

"Literacy... means far more than learning how to read and write... The aim is to transmit... knowledge and promote social participation."

- UNESCO

"Literacy is not a luxury, it is a right and a responsibility. If our world is to meet the challenges of the twenty-first century we must harness the energy and creativity of all our citizens."

- President Bill Clinton

"Parents should be encouraged to read to their children, and teachers should be equipped with all available techniques for teaching literacy, so the varying needs and capacities of individual kids can be taken into account."

- Hugh Mackay

CONTENTS

I

PONY'S MOTHER, AND WHY HE HAD
A RIGHT TO RUN OFF

If there was any fellow in the Boy's Town fifty years ago who had a good reason to run off it was Pony Baker. Pony was not his real name; it was what the boys called him, because there were so many fellows who had to be told apart, as Big Joe and Little Joe, and Big John and Little John, and Big Bill and Little Bill, that they got tired of telling boys apart that way; and after one of the boys called him Pony Baker, so that you could know him from his cousin Frank Baker, nobody ever called him anything else.

You would have known Pony from the other Frank Baker, anyway, if you had seen them together, for the other Frank Baker was a tall, lank, tow-headed boy, with a face so full of freckles that you could not have put a pin-point between them, and large, bony hands that came a long way out of his coat-sleeves; and the Frank Baker that I mean here was little and dark and round, with a thick crop of black hair on his nice head; and he had black eyes, and a smooth, swarthy face, without a freckle on it. He was pretty well dressed in clothes that fitted him, and his hands were small and plump. His legs were rather short, and he walked and ran with quick, nipping steps, just like a pony; and you would have thought of a pony when you looked at him, even if that had not been his nickname.

That very thing of his being dressed so well was one of the worst things that was done to him by his mother, who was always disgracing him before the other boys, though she may not have known it. She never was willing to have him go barefoot, and if she could she would have kept his shoes on him the whole summer; as it was, she did keep them on till all the other boys had been barefoot so long that their soles were as hard as horn; and they could walk on broken glass, or anything, and had stumped the nails off their big toes, and had grass cuts under their little ones, and yarn tied into them, before Pony Baker was allowed to take his shoes off in the spring. He would have taken them off and gone barefoot without his mother's knowing it, and many of the boys said that he ought to do it; but then she would have found it out by the look of his feet when he went to bed, and maybe told his father about it.

Very likely his father would not have cared so much; sometimes he would ask Pony's mother why she did not turn the boy barefoot with the other boys, and then she would ask Pony's father if he wanted the child to take his death of cold; and that would hush him up, for Pony once had a little brother that died.

Pony had nothing but sisters, after that, and this was another thing that kept him from having a fair chance with the other fellows. His mother wanted him to play with his sisters, and she did not care, or else she did not know, that a girl-boy was about the meanest thing there was, and that if you played with girls you could not help being a girl-boy. Pony liked to play with his sisters well enough when there were no boys around, but when there were his mother did not act as if she could not see any difference. The girls themselves were not

W. D. Howells

so bad, and they often coaxed their mother to let him go off with the other boys, when she would not have let him without. But even then, if it was going in swimming, or fishing, or skating before the ice was very thick, she would show that she thought he was too little to take care of himself, and would make some big boy promise that he would look after Pony; and all the time Pony would be gritting his teeth, he was so mad.

Once, when Pony stayed in swimming all day with a crowd of fellows, she did about the worst thing she ever did; she came down to the river-bank and stood there, and called to the boys, to find out if Pony was with them; and they all had to get into the water up to their necks before they could bear to answer her, they were so ashamed; and Pony had to put on his clothes and go home with her. He could see that she had been crying, and that made him a little sorry, but not so very; and the most that he was afraid of was that she would tell his father. But if she did he never knew it, and that night she came to him after he went to bed, and begged him so not to stay in swimming the whole day any more, and told him how frightened she had been, that he had to promise; and then that made him feel worse than ever, for he did not see how he could break his promise.

She was not exactly a bad mother, and she was not exactly a good mother. If she had been really a good mother she would have let him do whatever he wanted, and never made any trouble, and if she had been a bad mother she would not have let him do anything; and then he could have done it without her letting him. In some ways she was good enough; she would let him take out things to the boys in the back yard from the table, and she put apple-butter or molasses on when it was hot biscuit that he took out. Once she let him have a birthday party, and had cake and candy-pulling and lemonade, and nobody but boys, because he said that boys hated girls; even his own sisters did not come. Sometimes she would give him money for ice-cream, and if she could have got over being particular about his going in swimming before he could swim, and pistols and powder and such things, she would have done very well.

She was first-rate when he was sick, and nobody could take care of him like her, cooling his pillow and making the bed easy, and keeping everybody quiet; and when he began to get well she would cook things that tasted better than anything you ever knew: stewed chicken, and toast with gravy on, and things like that. Even when he was well, and just lonesome, she would sit by his bed if he asked her, till he went to sleep, or got quieted down; and if he was trying to make anything she would help him all she could, but if it was something that you had to use a knife with she was not much help.

It always seemed to Pony that she begrudged his going with the boys, and she said how nice he used to keep his clothes before, and had such pretty manners, and now he was such a sloven, and was so rude and fierce that she was almost afraid of him. He knew that she was making fun about being afraid of him; and if she did hate to have him go with some of the worst boys, still she was willing to help in lots of ways. She gave him yarn to make a ball with, and she covered it for him with leather. Sometimes she seemed to do things for him that she would not do for his sisters, and she often made them give up to him when they had a dispute.

She made a distinction between boys and girls, and did not make him help with the housework. Of course he had to bring in wood, but all the fellows had to do that, and they did not count it; what they hated was having to churn, or wipe dishes after company. Pony's mother never made him do anything like that; she said it was girls' work; and she would not let him learn to milk, either, for she said that milking was women's work, and all that Pony had to do with the cow was to bring her home from the pasture in the evening.

Sometimes when there was company she would let him bring in a boy to the second table, and she gave them all the preserves and cake that they could eat. The kind of company she had was what nearly all the mothers had in the Boy's Town; they asked a whole lot of other mothers to supper, and had stewed chicken and hot biscuit, and tea and coffee, and quince and peach preserves, and sweet tomato pickles, and cake with jelly in between, and pound-cake with frosting on, and buttered toast, and maybe fried eggs and ham. The fathers never seemed to come; or, if the father that belonged in the house came, he did not go and sit in the parlor with the mothers after supper, but went up-town, to the post-office, or to some of the lawyers' offices, or else a store, and talked politics.

Pony never thought his mother was good looking, or, rather, he did not think anything about that, and it always seemed to him that she must be a pretty old woman; but once when she had company, and she came in from the kitchen with the last dish, and put it on the table, one of the nicest of the other mothers came up, and put her arm around Pony's mother, and said:

"How pretty you do look, Mrs. Baker! I just want to kiss you on those red cheeks. I should say you were a girl, instead of having all those children."

Pony was standing out on the porch with his five sisters, and when he looked in through the door, and saw his mother with her head thrown back laughing, and her face flushed from standing over the stove to cook the supper, and her brown hair tossed a little, he did think that she was very nice looking, and like the girls at school that were in the fourth reader; and she was very nicely dressed, too, in a white muslin dress, with the blue check apron she had been working in flung behind the kitchen door, as she came into the sitting-room carrying the dish in one hand. He did not know what the other mother meant by saying "all those children"; for it was a small family for the Boy's Town, and he thought she must just be fooling.

Sometimes his mother would romp with the children, or sing them funny, old-fashioned songs, such as people used to sing when the country was first settled and everybody lived in log cabins. When she got into one of her joking times she would call Pony "Honey! Honey!" like the old colored aunty that had the persimmon-tree in her yard; and if she had to go past him she would wind her arm around his head and mumble the top of it with her lips; and if there were any of the fellows there, and Pony would fling her arm away because he hated to have her do it before them, she would just laugh.

Of course, if she had been a good mother about everything else Pony would not have minded that, but she was such a very bad mother about letting him have fun, sometimes, that Pony could not overlook it, as he might have done. He did not think that she ought to call him Pony before the boys, for, though he did not mind the boys' calling him Pony, it was not the thing for a fellow's mother, and it was sure to give them the notion she babied him at home. Once, after she called him "Pony, dear!" the fellows mocked her when they got away, and all of them called him "Pony, dear!" till he began to cry and to stone them.

But the worst of her ways was about powder, and her not wanting him to have it, or not wanting him to have it where there was fire. She would never let him come near the stove with it, after one of the fellows had tried to dry his powder on the stove when it had got wet from being pumped on in

W. D. Howells

his jacket-pocket while he was drinking at the pump, and the fellow forgot to take it off the stove quick enough, and it almost blew his mother up, and did pretty nearly scare her to death; and she would not let him keep it in a bottle, or anything, but just loose in a paper, because another of the fellows had begun to pour powder once from a bottle onto a coal of fire, and the fire ran up the powder, and blew the bottle to pieces, and filled the fellow's face so full of broken glass that the doctor was nearly the whole of that Fourth of July night getting it out. So, although she was a good mother in some things, she was a bad mother in others, and these were the great things; and they were what gave him the right to run off.

II

THE RIGHT THAT PONY HAD TO RUN OFF, FROM THE WAY HIS FATHER ACTED

Pony had a right to run off from some of the things that his father had done, but it seemed to him that they were mostly things that his mother had put his father up to, and that his father would not have been half as bad if he had been let alone. In the Boy's Town the fellows celebrated Christmas just as they did Fourth of July, by firing off pistols and shooting crackers, and one Christmas one of the fellows' pistols burst and blew the ball of his thumb open, and when a crowd of the fellows helped him past Pony's house, crying and limping (the pain seemed to go down his leg, and lame him), Pony's mother made his father take Pony's pistol right away from him, and not let him have it till after New Year's; and what made it worse was that Pony had faithfully kept his promise to her that he would not fire anything out of his pistol but paper wads, while all the other fellows were firing shot, and tacks, and little marbles, out of theirs; and some of them tried to shame him into breaking his word, and he had to stand their calling him cry-baby, and everything.

Then, she would not let his father get him a gun to go hunting with, because he would have to fire something besides wads out of that, and would be sure to kill himself.

Pony told her that he would not kill himself, and tried to laugh her out of the notion, but it was no use, and he never had a gun till he was twelve years old; he was nine at the time I mean. One of the fellows who was only eight was going to have a gun as soon as his brother got done with his.

She would hardly let his father get him a dog, and I suppose it was something but Pony's disappointment about the gun that made her agree to the dog at last; even then she would not agree to his having it before it had its eyes open, when the great thing about a puppy was its not having its eyes open, and it was fully two weeks old before he was allowed to bring it home, though he was taken to choose it before it could walk very well, and he went every day afterwards to see how it was getting along, and to watch out that it did not get changed with the other little dogs. The first night after he got it to his own house, the dog whined so with home-sickness that it kept everybody awake till Pony went to the woodshed, where it was in the clothes-basket, and took it into his own bed; then it went to sleep, and did not whine a bit. His father let him keep it there that one night, but the next he made him put it out again, because he said it would get the house full of fleas; and he said if it made much more trouble he would make Pony take it back.

He was not a very good father about money, because when Pony went to ask him for a five-cent piece he always wanted to know what it was for, and even when it was for a good thing a fellow did not always like to tell. If his father did not think it was a good thing he would not let Pony have it, and then Pony would be ashamed to go back to the boys, for they would say his father was stingy, though perhaps none of them had tried to get money from their own fathers.

Every now and then the fellows tried to learn to smoke, and that was a thing that Pony's father would not let him do. He would let him smoke the drift-wood twigs, which the boys picked up along the river shore and called smoke-wood, or he would let him smoke grapevine or the pods of the catalpa, which were just like cigars, but he was mean about real tobacco. Once, when he found a cigar in Pony's pocket, he threw it into the fire, and said that if he ever knew him to have another he would have a talk with him.

He was pretty bad about wanting Pony to weed his mother's flower-beds and about going regularly to school, and always getting up in time for school. To be sure, if a show or a circus came along, he nearly always took Pony in, but then he was apt to take the girls, too, and he did not like to have Pony go off with a crowd of boys, which was the only way to go into a show; for if the fellows saw you with your family, all dressed up, and maybe with your shoes on, they would make fun of you the next time they caught you out.

He made Pony come in every night before nine o'clock, and even Christmas Eve, or the night before Fourth of July, he would not let him stay up the whole night. When he went to the city, as the boys called the large town twenty miles away from the Boy's Town, he might get Pony a present or he might not, but he would not promise, because once when he promised, he forgot it, and then Pony's mother scolded him.

There were some boys' fathers in the Boy's Town who were good fathers, and let their children do whatever they pleased, and Pony could not help feeling rather ashamed before these boys. If one of that sort of fellows' fathers passed a crowd of boys, they would not take any notice of their boys; but if Pony's father came along, he would very likely say, "Well, Pony!" or something like that, and then all the fellows would hollo, "Well, Pony! Well, Pony!" and make fun of his father, when he got past, and walk like him, or something, so that Pony would be so mad he would hardly know what to do. He hated to ask his father not to speak to him, or look at him, when he was with the fellows, but it seemed to him as if his father ought to know better without asking.

There were a great many things like that which no good father would have done, but the thing that made Pony lose all patience, and begin getting ready to run off right away, was the way his father behaved when Pony got mad at the teacher one day, and brought his books home, and said he was not going back to that school any more. The reason was because the teacher had put Pony back from third reader to the second and made him go into a class of little fellows not more than seven years old. It happened one morning, after a day when Pony had read very badly in the afternoon, and though he had explained that he had read badly because the weather was so hot, the teacher said he might try it in the second reader till the weather changed, at any rate; and the whole school laughed. The worst of it was that Pony was really a very good reader, and could speak almost the best of any of the boys; but that afternoon he was lazy, and would not pay attention.

At recess, after the teacher had put him back, all the fellows came round and asked him what he was going to do now; and he just shut his teeth and told them they would see; and at noon they did see. As soon as school was dismissed, or even before, Pony put all his books together, and his slate, and tied them with his slate-pencil string, and twitched his hat down off the peg, and strutted proudly out of the room, so that not only the boys but the teacher, too, could see that he was leaving school. The teacher looked on and pretended to smile, but Pony did not smile; he kept his teeth shut, and walked stiffly through the door, and straight home, without speaking to any one. That was the way to do when you left school in the Boy's Town, for then the boys would know you were in earnest; and none of them would try to speak to you, either; they would respect you too much.

Pony's mother knew that he had left school as soon as she saw him bringing home his books, but she only looked sorry and did not say anything. She must have told his father about it when he came to dinner, though, for as soon as they sat down at the table his father began to ask what the trouble was. Pony answered very haughtily, and said that old Archer had put him back into the second reader, and he was not going to stand it, and he had left school.

"Then," said his father, "you expect to stay in the second reader the rest of your life?"

This was something that Pony had never thought of before; but he said he did not care, and he was not going to have old Archer put him back, anyway, and he began to cry.

It was then that his mother showed herself a good mother, if ever she was one, and said she thought it was a shame to put Pony back and mortify him before the other boys, and she knew that it must just have happened that he did not read very well that afternoon because he was sick, or something, for usually he read perfectly.

His father said, "My dear girl, my dear girl!" and his mother hushed up and did not say anything more; but Pony could see what she thought, and he accused old Archer of always putting on him and always trying to mortify him.

"That's all very well," said his father, "but I think we ought to give him one more trial; and I advise you to take your books back again this afternoon, and read so well that he will put you into the fourth reader to-morrow morning."

Pony understood that his father was just making fun about

W. D. Howells

the fourth reader, but was in earnest about his going back to school; and he left the table and threw himself on the lounge, with his face down, and cried. He said he was sick, and his head ached, and he could not go to school; his father said that he hoped his headache would wear off in the course of the afternoon, but if he was worse they would have the doctor when he came home from school.

Then he took his hat and went out of the front door to go up town, and Pony screamed out, "Well, I'll run off; that's what I'll do!"

His father did not take any notice of him, and his mother only said, "Pony, Pony!" while his sisters all stood round frightened at the way Pony howled and thrashed the lounge with his legs.

But before one o'clock Pony washed his face and brushed his hair, and took his books and started for school. His mother tried to kiss him, but he pushed her off, for it seemed to him that she might have made his father let him stay out of school, if she had tried, and he was not going to have any of her pretending. He made his face very cold and hard as he marched out of the house, for he never meant to come back to that house any more. He meant to go to school that afternoon, but as soon as school was out he was going to run off.

When the fellows saw him coming back with his books they knew how it was, but they did not mock him, for he had done everything that he could, and all that was expected of anybody in such a case. A boy always came back when he had left school in that way, and nobody supposed but what he would; the thing was to leave school; after that you were not to blame, whatever happened.

Before recess it began to be known among them that Pony was going to run off, because his father had made him come back, and then they did think he was somebody; and as soon as they got out at recess they all crowded round him and began to praise him up, and everything, and to tell him that they would run off, too, if their fathers sent them back; and so he began to be glad that he was going to do it. They asked him when he was going to run off, and he told them they would see; and pretty soon it was understood that he was going to run off the same night.

When school was out a whole crowd of them started with him, and some of the biggest fellows walked alongside of him, and talked down over their shoulders to him, and told him what he must do. They said he must not start till after dark, and he must watch out for the constable till he got over the corporation line and then nobody could touch him. They said that they would be waiting round the corner for him as soon as they had their suppers, and one of them would walk along with him to the end of the first street and then another would be waiting there to go with him to the end of the next, and so on till they reached the corporation line. Very likely his father would have the constable waiting there to stop him, but Pony ought to start to run across the line and then the fellows would rush out and trip up the constable and hold him down till Pony got safe across. He ought to hollo, when he was across, and that would let them know that he was safe and they would be ready to let the constable up, and begin to run before he could grab them.

Everybody thought that was a splendid plan except Archy Hawkins, that all the fellows called Old Hawkins; his father kept one of the hotels, and Old Hawkins used to catch frogs for the table; he was the one that the frogs used to know by sight, and when they saw him they would croak out: "Here comes Hawkins! Here comes Hawkins! Look out!" and jump

W. D. Howells

off the bank into the water and then come up among the green slime, where nobody but Old Hawkins could see them. He was always joking and getting into scrapes, but still the boys liked him and thought he was pretty smart, and now they did not mind it when he elbowed the big boys away that were talking to Pony and told them to shut up.

"You just listen to your uncle, Pony!" he said. "These fellows don't know anything about running off. I'll tell you how to do it; you mind your uncle! It's no use trying to get away from the constable, if he's there, for he'll catch you as quick as lightning, and he won't mind these fellows any more than fleas. You oughtn't try to start till along about midnight, for the constable will be in bed by that time, and you won't have any trouble. You must have somebody to wake you up, and some of the fellows ought to be outside, to do it. You listen to your grandfather! You ought to tie a string around your big toe, and let the string hang out of the window, the way you do Fourth of July eve; and then just as soon as it strikes twelve, the fellows ought to tug away at the string till you come hopping to the window, and tell 'em to stop. But you got to whisper, and the fellows mustn't make any noise, either, or your father will be out on them in a minute. He'll be watching out, to-night, anyway, I reckon, because—"

Old Hawkins was walking backward in front of Pony, talking to him, and showing him how he must hop to the window, and all at once he struck his heel against a root in the sidewalk, and the first thing he knew he sat down so hard that it about knocked the breath out of him.

All the fellows laughed, and anybody else would have been mad, but Old Hawkins was too good-natured; and he got up and brushed himself, and said: "Say! let's go down to the river and go in, before supper, anyway."

Nearly all the fellows agreed, and Old Hawkins said: "Come along, Pony! You got to come, too!"

But Pony stiffly refused, partly because it seemed to him pretty mean to forget all about his running away, like that, and partly because he had to ask his mother before he went in swimming. A few of the little fellows kept with him all the way home, but most of the big boys went along with Old Hawkins.

One of them stayed with Pony and the little boys, and comforted him for the way the rest had left him. He was a fellow who was always telling about Indians, and he said that if Pony could get to the Indians, anywhere, and they took a fancy to him, they would adopt him into their tribe, if it was just after some old chief had lost a son in battle. Maybe they would offer to kill him first, and they would have to hold a council, but if they did adopt him, it would be the best thing, because then he would soon turn into an Indian himself, and forget how to speak English; and if ever the Indians had to give up their prisoners, and he was brought back, and his father and mother came to pick him out, they might know him by some mark or other, but he would not know them, and they would have to let him go back to the Indians again. He said that was the very best way, and the only way, but the trouble would be to get to the Indians in the first place. He said he knew of one reservation in the north part of the State, and he promised to find out if there were any other Indians living nearer; the reservation was about a hundred miles off, and it would take Pony a good while to go to them.

The name of this boy was Jim Leonard. But now, before I go the least bit further with the story of Pony Baker's running away, I have got to tell about Jim Leonard, and what kind of boy he was, and the scrape that he once got Pony and the other boys into, and a hair-breadth escape he had himself, when he came pretty near being drowned in a freshet; and I will begin with the hair-breadth escape, because it happened before the scrape.

III

JIM LEONARD'S HAIR-BREADTH ESCAPE

Jim Leonard's stable used to stand on the flat near the river, and on a rise of ground above it stood Jim Leonard's log-cabin. The boys called it Jim Leonard's log-cabin, but it was really his mother's, and the stable was hers, too. It was a log stable, but up where the gable began the logs stopped, and it was weather-boarded the rest of the way, and the roof was shingled.

Jim Leonard said it was all logs once, and that the roof was loose clap-boards, held down by logs that ran across them, like the roofs in the early times, before there were shingles or nails, or anything, in the country. But none of the oldest boys had ever seen it like that, and you had to take Jim Leonard's word for it if you wanted to believe it. The little fellows nearly all did; but everybody said afterwards it was a good thing for Jim Leonard that it was not that kind of roof when he had his hair-breadth escape on it. He said himself that he would not have cared if it had been; but that was when it was all over, and his mother had whipped him, and everything, and he was telling the boys about it.

He said that in his Pirate Book lots of fellows on rafts got to land when they were shipwrecked, and that the old-fashioned

　W. D. Howells

roof would have been just like a raft, anyway, and he could have steered it right across the river to Delorac's Island as easy! Pony Baker thought very likely he could, but Hen Billard said:

"Well, why didn't you do it, with the kind of a roof you had?"

Some of the boys mocked Jim Leonard; but a good many of them thought he could have done it if he could have got into the eddy that there was over by the island. If he could have landed there, once, he could have camped out and lived on fish till the river fell.

It was that spring, about fifty-four years ago, when the freshet, which always came in the spring, was the worst that anybody could remember. The country above the Boy's Town was under water, for miles and miles. The river bottoms were flooded so that the corn had to be all planted over again when the water went down. The freshet tore away pieces of orchard, and apple-trees in bloom came sailing along with logs and fence rails and chicken-coops, and pretty soon dead cows and horses. There was a dog chained to a dog-kennel that went by, howling awfully; the boys would have given anything if they could have saved him, but the yellow river whirled him out of sight behind the middle pier of the bridge, which everybody was watching from the bank, expecting it to go any minute. The water was up within four or five feet of the bridge, and the boys believed that if a good big log had come along and hit it, the bridge would have been knocked loose from its piers and carried down the river.

Perhaps it would, and perhaps it would not. The boys all ran to watch it as soon as school was out, and stayed till they had to go to supper. After supper some of their mothers let them come back and stay till bedtime, if they would promise to keep a full yard back from the edge of the bank. They could not be sure just how much a yard was, and they nearly all sat down on the edge and let their legs hang over.

Jim Leonard was there, holloing and running up and down the bank, and showing the other boys things away out in the river that nobody else could see; he said he saw a man out there. He had not been to supper, and he had not been to school all day, which might have been the reason why he would rather stay with the men and watch the bridge than go home to supper; his mother would have been waiting for him with a sucker from the pear-tree. He told the boys that while they were gone he went out with one of the men on the bridge as far as the middle pier, and it shook like a leaf; he showed with his hand how it shook.

Jim Leonard was a fellow who believed he did all kinds of things that he would like to have done; and the big boys just laughed. That made Jim Leonard mad, and he said that as soon as the bridge began to go, he was going to run out on it and go with it; and then they would see whether he was a liar or not! They mocked him and danced round him till he cried. But Pony Baker, who had come with his father, believed that Jim Leonard would really have done it; and at any rate, he felt sorry for him when Jim cried.

He stayed later than any of the little fellows, because his father was with him, and even all the big boys had gone home except Hen Billard, when Pony left Jim Leonard on the bank and stumbled sleepily away, with his hand in his father's.

When Pony was gone, Hen Billard said: "Well, going to stay all night, Jim?"

And Jim Leonard answered back, as cross as could be, "Yes,

I am!" And he said the men who were sitting up to watch the bridge were going to give him some of their coffee, and that would keep him awake. But perhaps he thought this because he wanted some coffee so badly. He was awfully hungry, for he had not had anything since breakfast, except a piece of bread-and-butter that he got Pony Baker to bring him in his pocket when he came down from school at noontime.

Hen Billard said, "Well, I suppose I won't see you any more, Jim; good-bye," and went away laughing; and after a while one of the men saw Jim Leonard hanging about, and asked him what he wanted there, at that time of night; and Jim could not say he wanted coffee, and so there was nothing for him to do but go. There was nowhere for him to go but home, and he sneaked off in the dark.

When he came in sight of the cabin he could not tell whether he would rather have his mother waiting for him with a whipping and some supper, or get to bed somehow with neither. He climbed softly over the back fence and crept up to the back door, but it was fast; then he crept round to the front door, and that was fast, too. There was no light in the house, and it was perfectly still.

All of a sudden it struck him that he could sleep in the stable-loft, and he thought what a fool he was not to have thought of it before. The notion brightened him up so that he got the gourd that hung beside the well-curb and took it out to the stable with him; for now he remembered that the cow would be there, unless she was in somebody's garden-patch or corn-field.

He noticed as he walked down towards the stable that the freshet had come up over the flat, and just before the door he had to wade. But he was in his bare feet and he did not care; if he thought anything, he thought that his mother would not come out to milk till the water went down, and he would be safe till then from the whipping he must take, sooner or later, for playing hooky.

Sure enough, the old cow was in the stable, and she gave Jim Leonard a snort of welcome and then lowed anxiously. He fumbled through the dark to her side, and began to milk her. She had been milked only a few hours before, and so he got only a gourdful from her. But it was all strippings, and rich as cream, and it was smoking warm. It seemed to Jim Leonard that it went down to his very toes when he poured it into his throat, and it made him feel so good that he did not know what to do.

There really was not anything for him to do but to climb up into the loft by the ladder in the corner of the stable, and lie down on the old last year's fodder. The rich, warm milk made Jim Leonard awfully sleepy, and he dropped off almost as soon as his head touched the corn-stalks. The last thing he remembered was the hoarse roar of the freshet outside, and that was a lulling music in his ears.

The next thing he knew, and he hardly knew that, was a soft, jolting, sinking motion, first to one side and then to another; then he seemed to be going down, down, straight down, and then to be drifting off into space. He rubbed his eyes, and found it was full daylight, although it was the daylight of early morning; and while he lay looking out of the stable-loft window and trying to make out what it all meant, he felt a wash of cold water along his back, and his bed of fodder melted away under him and around him, and some loose planks of the loft floor swam weltering out of the window. Then he knew what had happened. The flood had stolen up while he slept, and sapped the walls of the stable; the logs had given way, one after another, and had let him down, with the roof, into the water.

　　　　　W. D. Howells

He got to his feet as well as he could, and floundered over the rising and falling boards to the window in the floating gable. One look outside showed him his mother's log-cabin safe on its rise of ground, and at the corner the old cow, that must have escaped through the stable door he had left open, and passed the night among the cabbages. She seemed to catch sight of Jim Leonard when he put his head out, and she lowed to him.

Jim Leonard did not stop to make any answer. He clambered out of the window and up onto the ridge of the roof, and there, in the company of a large gray rat, he set out on the strangest voyage a boy ever made. In a few moments the current swept him out into the middle of the river, and he was sailing down between his native shore on one side and Delorac's Island on the other.

All round him seethed and swirled the yellow flood in eddies and ripples, where drift of all sorts danced and raced. His vessel, such as it was, seemed seaworthy enough. It held securely together, fitting like a low, wide cup over the water, and perhaps finding some buoyancy from the air imprisoned in it above the window. But Jim Leonard was not satisfied, and so far from being proud of his adventure, he was frightened worse even than the rat which shared it. As soon as he could get his voice, he began to shout for help to the houses on the empty shores, which seemed to fly backward on both sides while he lay still on the gulf that swashed around him, and tried to drown his voice before it swallowed him up. At the same time the bridge, which had looked so far off when he first saw it, was rushing swiftly towards him, and getting nearer and nearer.

He wondered what had become of all the people and all the boys. He thought that if he were safe there on shore he should not be sleeping in bed while somebody was out in the river on a roof, with nothing but a rat to care whether he got drowned or not.

Where was Hen Billard, that always made fun so; or Archy Hawkins, that pretended to be so good-natured; or Pony Baker, that seemed to like a fellow so much? He began to call for them by name: "Hen Billard—*O* Hen! Help, help! Archy Hawkins, *O* Archy! I'm drowning! Pony, Pony, *O* Pony! Don't you see me, Pony?"

He could see the top of Pony Baker's house, and he thought what a good, kind man Pony's father was. Surely *he* would try to save him; and Jim Leonard began to yell: "O Mr. Baker! Look here, Mr. Baker! It's Jim Leonard, and I'm floating down the river on a roof! Save me, Mr. Baker, save me! Help, help, somebody! Fire! Fire! Fire! Murder! Fire!"

By this time he was about crazy, and did not half know what he was saying. Just in front of where Hen Billard's grand-mother lived, on the street that ran along the top of the bank, the roof got caught in the branches of a tree which had drifted down and stuck in the bottom of the river so that the branches waved up and down as the current swashed through them. Jim Leonard was glad of anything that would stop the roof, and at first he thought he would get off on the tree. That was what the rat did. Perhaps the rat thought Jim Leonard really was crazy and he had better let him have the roof to himself; but the rat saw that he had made a mistake, and he jumped back again after he had swung up and down on a limb two or three times. Jim Leonard felt awfully when the rat first got into the tree, for he remembered how it said in the Pirate Book that rats always leave a sinking ship, and now he believed that he certainly was gone. But that only made him hollo the louder, and he holloed so loud that at last he made somebody hear.

W. D. Howells

It was Hen Billard's grandmother, and she put her head out of the window with her night-cap on, to see what the matter was. Jim Leonard caught sight of her and he screamed, "Fire, fire, fire! I'm drownding, Mrs. Billard! Oh, do somebody come!"

Hen Billard's grandmother just gave one yell of "Fire! The world's a-burnin' up, Hen Billard, and you layin' there sleepin' and not helpin' a bit! Somebody's out there in the river!" and she rushed into the room where Hen was, and shook him.

He bounced out of bed and pulled on his pantaloons, and was down-stairs in a minute. He ran bareheaded over to the bank, and when Jim Leonard saw him coming he holloed ten times as loud: "It's me, Hen! It's Jim Leonard! Oh, do get somebody to come out and save me! Fire!"

As soon as Hen heard that, and felt sure it was not a dream, which he did in about half a second, he began to yell, too, and to say: "How did you get there? Fire, fire, fire! What are you on? Fire! Are you in a tree, or what? Fire, fire! Are you in a flat-boat? Fire, fire, fire! If I had a skiff—fire!"

He kept racing up and down the bank, and back and forth between the bank and the houses. The river was almost up to the top of the bank, and it looked a mile wide. Down at the bridge you could hardly see any light between the water and the bridge.

Pretty soon people began to look out of their doors and windows, and Hen Billard's grandmother kept screaming, "The world's a-burnin' up! The river's on fire!" Then boys came out of their houses; and then men with no hats on; and then women and girls, with their hair half down. The fire-bells began to ring, and in less than five minutes both the fire companies were on the shore, with the men at the brakes and the foremen of the companies holloing through their trumpets.

Then Jim Leonard saw what a good thing it was that he had thought of holloing fire. He felt sure now that they would save him somehow, and he made up his mind to save the rat, too, and pet it, and maybe go around and exhibit it. He would name it Bolivar; it was just the color of the elephant Bolivar that came to the Boy's Town every year. These things whirled through his brain while he watched two men setting out in a skiff towards him.

They started from the shore a little above him, and they meant to row slanting across to his tree, but the current, when they got fairly into it, swept them far below, and they were glad to row back to land again without ever getting anywhere near him. At the same time, the tree-top where his roof was caught was pulled southward by a sudden rush of the torrent; it opened, and the roof slipped out, with Jim Leonard and the rat on it. They both joined in one squeal of despair as the river leaped forward with them, and a dreadful "Oh!" went up from the people on the bank.

Some of the firemen had run down to the bridge when they saw that the skiff was not going to be of any use, and one of them had got out of the window of the bridge onto the middle pier, with a long pole in his hand. It had an iron hook at the end, and it was the kind of pole that the men used to catch drift-wood with and drag it ashore. When the people saw Blue Bob with that pole in his hand, they understood what he was up to. He was going to wait till the water brought the roof with Jim Leonard on it down to the bridge, and then catch the hook into the shingles and pull it up to the pier. The strongest current set close in around the middle pier, and the roof would have to pass on one side or the

W. D. Howells

other. That was what Blue Bob argued out in his mind when he decided that the skiff would never reach Jim Leonard, and he knew that if he could not save him that way, nothing could save him.

Blue Bob must have had a last name, but none of the little fellows knew what it was. Everybody called him Blue Bob because he had such a thick, black beard that when he was just shaved his face looked perfectly blue. He knew all about the river and its ways, and if it had been of any use to go out with a boat, he would have gone. That was what all the boys said, when they followed Blue Bob to the bridge and saw him getting out on the pier. He was the only person that the watchman had let go on the bridge for two days.

The water was up within three feet of the floor, and if Jim Leonard's roof slipped by Blue Bob's guard and passed under the bridge, it would scrape Jim Leonard off, and that would be the last of him.

All the time the roof was coming nearer the bridge, sometimes slower, sometimes faster, just as it got into an eddy or into the current; once it seemed almost to stop, and swayed completely round; then it just darted forward.

Blue Bob stood on the very point of the pier, where the strong stone-work divided the current, and held his hooked pole ready to make a clutch at the roof, whichever side it took. Jim Leonard saw him there, but although he had been holloing and yelling and crying all the time, now he was still. He wanted to say, "O Bob, save me!" but he could not make a sound.

It seemed to him that Bob was going to miss him when he made a lunge at the roof on the right side of the pier; it seemed to him that the roof was going down the left side; but he felt it quiver and stop, and then it gave a loud crack and went to pieces, and flung itself away upon the whirling and dancing flood. At first Jim Leonard thought he had gone with it; but it was only the rat that tried to run up Blue Bob's pole, and slipped off into the water; and then somehow Jim was hanging onto Blue Bob's hands and scrambling onto the bridge.

Blue Bob always said he never saw any rat, and a good many people said there never was any rat on the roof with Jim Leonard; they said that he just made the rat up.

He did not mention the rat himself for several days; he told Pony Baker that he did not think of it at first, he was so excited.

Pony asked his father what he thought, and Pony's father said that it might have been the kind of rat that people see when they have been drinking too much, and that Blue Bob had not seen it because he had signed the temperance pledge.

But this was a good while after. At the time the people saw Jim Leonard standing safe with Blue Bob on the pier, they set up a regular election cheer, and they would have believed anything Jim Leonard said. They all agreed that Blue Bob had a right to go home with Jim and take him to his mother, for he had saved Jim's life, and he ought to have the credit of it.

Before this, and while everybody supposed that Jim Leonard would surely be drowned, some of the people had gone up to his mother's cabin to prepare her for the worst. She did not seem to understand exactly, and she kept round getting breakfast, with her old clay pipe in her mouth; but when she got it through her head, she made an awful face, and dropped her pipe on the door-stone and broke it; and then she threw

W. D. Howells

her check apron over her head and sat down and cried.

But it took so long for her to come to this that the people had not got over comforting her and trying to make her believe that it was all for the best, when Blue Bob came up through the bars with his hand on Jim's shoulder, and about all the boys in town tagging after them.

Jim's mother heard the hurrahing and pulled off her apron, and saw that Jim was safe and sound there before her. She gave him a look that made him slip round behind Blue Bob, and she went in and got a table-knife, and she came out and went to the pear-tree and cut a sucker.

She said, "I'll learn that limb to sleep in a cow-barn when he's got a decent bed in the house!" and then she started to come towards Jim Leonard.

IV

THE SCRAPE THAT JIM LEONARD
GOT THE BOYS INTO

As I said, it was in the spring that Jim Leonard's hair-breadth escape happened. But it was late in the summer of that very same year that he got Pony Baker and all the rest of the boys into about one of the worst scrapes that the Boy's Town boys were ever in.

At first, it was more like a dare than anything else, for when Jim Leonard said he knew a watermelon patch that the owner had no use for, the other boys dared him to tell where it was. He wagged his head, and said that he knew, and then they dared him to tell whose patch it was; and all at once he said it was Bunty Williams's, and dared them to come and get the melons with him. None of the boys in the Boy's Town would take a dare, and so they set off with Jim Leonard, one sunny Saturday morning in September.

Some of the boys had their arms round one another's necks, talking as loud as they could into one another's faces, and some whooping and holloing, and playing Indian, and some throwing stones and scaring cats. They had nearly as many dogs as there were boys, and there were pretty nearly all the boys in the neighborhood. There seemed to be thirty or forty

W. D. Howells

of them, they talked so loud and ran round so, but perhaps there were only ten or eleven. Hen Billard was along, and so were Piccolo Wright and Archie Hawkins, and then a great lot of little fellows.

Pony Baker was not quite a little fellow in age; and there was something about him that always made the big boys let him go with their crowd. But now, when they passed Pony's gate and his mother saw them, and because it was such a warm morning and she thought they might be going down to the river and called out to him, "You mustn't go in swimming, Pony, dear; you'll get the ague," they began to mock Pony as soon as they got by, and to hollo, "No, Pony, dear! You mustn't get the ague. Keep out of the water if you don't want your teeth to rattle, Pony, dear!"

This made Pony so mad that he began to cry and try to fight them, and they all formed in a ring round him and danced and whooped till he broke through and started home. Then they ran after him and coaxed him not to do it, and said that they were just in fun. After that they used Pony first-rate, and he kept on with them.

Jim Leonard was at the head, walking along and holloing to the fellows to hurry up. They had to wade the river, and he was showing off how he could hop, skip, and jump through, when he stepped on a slippery stone and sat down in the water and made the fellows laugh. But they acted first-rate with him when they got across; they helped him to take off his trousers and wring them out, and they wrung them so hard that they tore them a little, but they were a little torn already; and they wrung them so dry that he said they felt splendid when he got them on again. One of his feet went through the side of the trouser leg that was torn before it got to the end, and made the fellows laugh.

When the boys first started Jim said he had got to go ahead so as to be sure that they found the right patch. He now said that Bunty Williams had two patches, one that he was going to sell the melons out of, and the other that he was going to let them go to seed in; and it was the second melon patch that he had deserted.

But pretty soon after they got over the river he came back and walked with the rest of the boys, and when they came to a piece of woods which they had to go through, he dropped behind. He said it was just the place for Indian, and he wanted to be where he could get at them if they started up when the boys got by, as they would very likely do.

Some of the big fellows called him a cowardy-calf; but he said he would show them when the time came, and most of the little boys believed him and tried to get in front. It was not long before he stopped and asked, What if he could not find the right patch? But the big boys said that they reckoned he could if he looked hard enough, and they made him keep on.

One of the dogs treed a squirrel, and Jim offered to climb the tree and shake the squirrel off; but Hen Billard said his watermelon tooth was beginning to trouble him, and he had no time for squirrels. That made all the big boys laugh, and they pulled Jim Leonard along, although he held back with all his might and told them to quit it. He began to cry.

Pony Baker did not know what to make of him. He felt sorry for him, but it seemed to him that Jim was acting as if he wanted to get out of showing the fellows where the patch was. Pony lent him his handkerchief, and Jim said that he had the toothache, anyway. He showed Pony the tooth, and the fellows saw him and made fun, and they offered to carry him, if his tooth ached so that he could not walk, and then suddenly Jim rushed ahead of the whole crowd.

They thought he was trying to run away from them, and two or three of the big fellows took after him, and when they caught up with him, the rest of the boys could see him pointing, and then the big boys that were with him gave a whoop and waved their hats, and all the rest of the boys tore along and tried which could run the fastest and get to the place the soonest.

They knew it must be something great; and sure enough it was a watermelon patch of pretty near an acre, sloping to the south from the edge of the woods, and all overrun with vines and just bulging all over with watermelons and muskmelons.

The watermelons were some of the big mottled kind, with lightish blotches among their darker green, like Georgia melons nowadays, and some almost striped in gray and green, and some were those big, round sugar melons, nearly black. They were all sizes, but most of them were large, and you need not "punk" them to see if they were ripe. Anybody could tell that they were ripe from looking at them, and the muskmelons, which were the old-fashioned long kind, were yellow as gold.

Now, the big fellows said, you could see why Bunty Williams had let this patch go to seed. It was because they were such bully melons and would have the best seeds; and the fellows all agreed to save the seeds for Bunty, and put them where he could find them. They began to praise Jim Leonard up, but he did not say anything, and only looked on with his queer, sleepy eyes, and said his tooth ached, when the fellows plunged down among the melons and began to burst them open.

They had lots of fun. At first they cut a few melons open

with their knives, but that was too slow, and pretty soon they began to jump on them and split them with sharp-edged rocks, or anything, to get them open quick. They did not eat close to the rind, as you do when you have a melon on the table, but they tore out the core and just ate that; and in about a minute they forgot all about saving the seeds for Bunty Williams and putting them in one place where he could get them.

Some of the fellows went into the edge of the woods to eat their melons, and then came back for more; some took them and cracked them open on the top rail of the fence, and then sat down in the fence corner and plunged their fists in and tore the cores out. Some of them squeezed the juice out of the cores into the shells of the melons and then drank it out of them.

Piccolo Wright was stooping over to pull a melon and Archie Hawkins came up behind him with a big melon that had a seam across it, it was so ripe; and he brought it down on Piccolo's head, and it smashed open and went all over Piccolo. He was pretty mad at first, but then he saw the fun of it, and he took one end of the melon and scooped it all out, and put it on in place of his hat and wore it like a helmet. Archie did the same thing with the other end, and then all the big boys scooped out melons and wore them for helmets. They were all drabbled with seeds and pulp, and some of the little fellows were perfectly soaked. None of them cared very much for the muskmelons.

Somehow Pony would not take any of the melons, although there was nothing that he liked so much. The fellows seemed to be having an awfully good time, and yet somehow it looked wrong to Pony. He knew that Bunty Williams had given up the patch, because Jim Leonard said so, and he knew that the boys had a right to the melons if Bunty had got

W. D. Howells

done with them; but still the sight of them there, smashing and gorging, made Pony feel anxious. It almost made him think that Jim Leonard was better than the rest because he would not take any of the melons, but stayed off at one side of the patch near the woods, where Pony stood with him.

He did not say much, and Pony noticed that he kept watching the log cabin where Bunty Williams lived on the slope of the hill about half a mile off, and once he heard Jim saying, as if to himself: "No, there isn't any smoke coming out of the chimbly, and that's a sign there ain't anybody there. They've all gone to market, I reckon."

It went through Pony that it was strange Jim should care whether Bunty was at home or not, if Bunty had given up the patch, but he did not say anything; it often happened so with him about the things he thought strange.

The fellows did not seem to notice where he was or what he was doing; they were all whooping and holloing, and now they began to play war with the watermelon rinds. One of the dogs thought he smelled a ground-squirrel and began to dig for it, and in about half a minute all the dogs seemed to be fighting, and the fellows were yelling round them and sicking them on; and they were all making such a din that Pony could hardly hear himself think, as his father used to say. But he thought he saw some one come out of Bunty's cabin, and take down the hill with a dog after him and a hoe in his hand.

He made Jim Leonard look, and Jim just gave a screech that rose above the din of the dogs and the other boys, "Bunty's coming, and he's got his bulldog and his shotgun!" And then he turned and broke through the woods.

All the boys stood still and stared at the hill-side, while the dogs fought on. The next thing they knew they were floundering among the vines and over the watermelon cores and shells and breaking for the woods; and as soon as the dogs found the boys were gone, they seemed to think it was no use to keep on fighting with nobody to look on, and they took after the fellows.

The big fellows holloed to the little fellows to come on, and the little fellows began crying. They caught their feet in the roots and dead branches and kept falling down, and some of the big fellows that were clever, like Hen Billard and Archie Hawkins, came back and picked them up and started them on again.

Nobody stopped to ask himself or any one else why they should be afraid of Bunty if he had done with his melon patch, but they all ran as if he had caught them stealing his melons, and had a right to shoot them, or set his dog on them.

They got through the woods to the shore of the river, and all the time they could hear Bunty Williams roaring and shouting, and Bunty Williams's bulldog barking, and it seemed as if he were right behind them. After they reached the river they had to run a long way up the shore before they got to the ripple where they could wade it, and by that time they were in such a hurry that they did not stop to turn up their trousers' legs; they just splashed right in and splashed across the best way they could. Some of them fell down, but everybody had to look out for himself, and they did not know that they were all safe over till they counted up on the other side.

Everybody was there but Jim Leonard, and they did not know what had become of him, but they were not very anxious. In fact they were all talking at the tops of their voices, and bragging what they would have done if Bunty had caught them.

Piccolo Wright showed how he could have tripped him up, and Archie Hawkins said that snuff would make a bulldog loosen his grip, because he would have to keep sneezing. None of them seemed to have seen either Bunty's shotgun or his bulldog, but they all believed that he had them because Jim Leonard said so, just as they had believed that Bunty had got done with his melon patch, until all at once one of them said, "Where is Jim Leonard, anyway?"

Then they found out that nobody knew, and the little fellows began to think that maybe Bunty Williams had caught him, but Hen Billard said: "Oh, he's safe enough, somewheres. I wish I had him here!"

Archie Hawkins asked, "What would you do to him?" and Hen said: "I'd show you! I'd make him go back and find out whether Bunty really had a bulldog with him. I don't believe he had."

Then all the big boys said that none of them believed so, either, and that they would bet that any of their dogs could whip Bunty's dog.

Their dogs did not look much like fighting. They were wet with running through the river, and they were lying round with their tongues hanging out, panting. But it made the boys think that something ought to be done to Jim Leonard, if they could ever find him, and some one said that they ought to look for him right away, but the rest said they ought to stop and dry their pantaloons first.

Pony began to be afraid they were going to hurt Jim Leonard if they got hold of him, and he said he was going home; and the boys tried to keep him from doing it. They said they were just going to build a drift-wood fire and dry their clothes at it, and they told him that if he went off in his wet trousers he would be sure to get the ague. But nothing that the boys could do would keep him, and so the big fellows said to let him go if he wanted to so much; and he climbed the river bank and left them kindling a fire.

When he got away and looked back, all the boys had their clothes off and were dancing round the fire like Indians, and he would have liked to turn back after he got to the top, and maybe he might have done so if he had not found Jim Leonard hiding in a hole up there and peeping over at the boys. Jim was crying, and said his tooth ached awfully, and he was afraid to go home and get something to put in it, because his mother would whale him as soon as she caught him.

He said he was hungry, too, and he wanted Pony to go over into a field with him and get a turnip, but Pony would not do it. He had three cents in his pocket—the big old kind that were as large as half-dollars and seemed to buy as much in that day—and he offered to let Jim take them and go and get something to eat at the grocery.

They decided he should buy two smoked red herrings and a cent's worth of crackers, and these were what Jim brought back after he had been gone so long that Pony thought he would never come. He had stopped to get some apples off one of the trees at his mother's house, and he had to watch his chance so that she should not see him, and then he had stopped and taken some potatoes out of a hill that would be first-rate if they could get some salt to eat them with, after they had built a fire somewhere and baked them.

They thought it would be a good plan to dig one of these

W. D. Howells

little caves just under the edge of the bank, and make a hole in the top to let the smoke out; but they would have to go a good way off so that the other fellows could not see them, and they could not wait for that. They divided the herrings between them, and they each had two crackers and three apples, and they made a good meal.

Then they went to a pump at the nearest house, where the woman said they might have a drink, and drank themselves full. They wanted awfully to ask her for some salt, but they did not dare to do it for fear she would make them tell what they wanted it for. So they came away without, and Jim said they could put ashes on their potatoes the way the Indians did, and it would be just as good as salt.

They ran back to the river bank, and ran along up it till they were out of sight of the boys on the shore below, and then they made their oven in it, and started their fire with some matches that Jim Leonard had in his pocket, so that if he ever got lost in the woods at night he could make a fire and keep from freezing. His tooth had stopped aching now, and he kept telling such exciting stories about Indians that Pony could not seem to get the chance to ask why Bunty Williams should take after the boys with his shotgun and bulldog if he had given up the watermelon patch and only wanted it for seed.

The question lurked in Pony's mind all the time that they were waiting for the potatoes to bake, but somehow he could not get it out. He did not feel very well, and he tried to forget his bad feelings by listening as hard as he could to Jim Leonard's stories. Jim kept taking the potatoes out to see if they were done enough, and he began to eat them while they were still very hard and greenish under the skin. Pony ate them, too, although he was not hungry now, and he did not think the ashes were as good as salt on them, as Jim pretended. The potato he ate seemed to make him feel no better, and at last he had to tell Jim that he was afraid he was going to be sick.

Jim said that if they could heat some stones, and get a blanket anywhere, and put it over Pony and the stones, and then pour water on the hot stones, they could give him a steam bath the way the Indians did, and it would cure him in a minute; they could get the stones easy enough, and he could bring water from the river in his straw hat, but the thing of it was to get the blanket.

He stood looking thoughtfully down at Pony, who was crying now, and begging Jim Leonard to go home with him, for he did not believe he could walk on account of the pain that seemed to curl him right up. He asked Jim if he believed he was beginning to have the ague, but Jim said it was more like the yellow janders, although he agreed that Pony had better go home, for it was pretty late, anyway.

He made Pony promise that if he would take him home he would let him get a good way off before he went into the house, so that Pony's father and mother should not see who had brought him. He said that when he had got off far enough he would hollo, and then Pony could go in. He was first-rate to Pony on the way home, and helped him to walk, and when the pain curled him up so tight that he could not touch his foot to the ground, Jim carried him.

Pony could never know just what to make of Jim Leonard. Sometimes he was so good to you that you could not help thinking he was one of the cleverest fellows in town, and then all of a sudden he would do something mean. He acted the perfect coward at times, and at other times he was not afraid of anything. Almost any of the fellows could whip him, but once he went into an empty house that was haunted, and came and looked out of the garret windows, and dared any of them to come up.

He offered now, if Pony did not want to go home and let his folks find out about the melon patch, to take him to his mother's log-barn, and get a witch-doctor to come and tend him; but Pony said that he thought they had better keep on, and then Jim trotted and asked him if the jolting did not do him some good. He said he just wished there was an Indian medicine-man around somewhere.

They were so long getting to Pony's house that it was almost dusk when they reached the back of the barn, and Jim put him over the fence. Jim started to run, and Pony waited till he got out of sight and holloed; then he began to shout, "Father! Mother! *O* mother! Come out here! I'm sick!"

It did not seem hardly a second till he heard his mother calling back: "Pony! Pony! Where are you, child? Where are you?"

"Here, behind the barn!" he answered.

Pony's mother came running out, and then his father, and when they had put him into his own bed up-stairs, his mother made his father go for the doctor. While his father was gone, his mother got the whole story out of Pony—what he had been doing all day, and what he had been eating—but as to who had got him into the trouble, she said she knew from the start it must be Jim Leonard.

After the doctor came and she told him what Pony had been eating, without telling all that he had been doing, the doctor gave him something to make him feel better. As soon as he said he felt better she began to talk very seriously to him, and to tell him how anxious she had been ever since she had seen him going off in the morning with Jim Leonard at the head of that crowd of boys.

"Didn't you know he couldn't be telling the truth when he said the man had left his watermelon patch? Didn't any of the boys?"

"No," said Pony, thoughtfully.

"But when he pretended that he shouldn't know the right patch, and wanted to turn back?"

"We didn't think anything. We thought he just wanted to get out of going. Ought they let him turn back? Maybe he meant to keep the patch all to himself."

His mother was silent, and Pony asked, "Do you believe that a boy has a right to take anything off a tree or a vine?"

"No; certainly not."

"Well, that's what I think, too."

"Why, Pony," said his mother, "is there anybody who thinks such a thing can be right?"

"Well, the boys say it's not stealing. Stealing is hooking a thing out of a wagon or a store; but if you can knock a thing off a tree, or get it through a fence, when it's on the ground already, then it's just like gathering nuts in the woods. That's what the boys say. Do you think it is?"

"I think it's the worst kind of stealing. I hope my boy doesn't do such things."

"Not very often," answered Pony, thoughtfully. "When

W. D. Howells

there's a lot of fellows together, you don't want them to laugh at you."

"O Pony, dear!" said his mother, almost crying.

"Well, anyway, mother," Pony said, to cheer her up, "I didn't take any of the watermelons to-day, for all Jim said Bunty had got done with them."

"I'm so glad to think you didn't! And you must promise, won't you, never to touch any fruit that doesn't belong to you?"

"But supposing an apple was to drop over the fence onto the sidewalk, what would you do then?"

"I should throw it right back over the fence again," said Pony's mother.

Pony promised his mother never to touch other people's fruit, but he was glad she did not ask him to throw it back over the fence if it fell outside, for he knew the fellows would laugh.

His father came back from going down-stairs with the doctor, and she told him all that Pony had told her, and it seemed to Pony that his father could hardly keep from laughing. But his mother did not even smile.

"How could Jim Leonard tell them that a man would give up his watermelon patch, and how could they believe such a lie, poor, foolish boys?"

"They wished to believe it," said Pony's father, "and so did Jim, I dare say."

"He might have got some of them killed, if Bunty Williams

had fired his gun at them," said Pony's mother; and he could see that she was not half-satisfied with what his father said.

"Perhaps it was a hoe, after all. You can't shoot anybody with a hoe-handle, and there is nothing to prove that it was a gun but Jim's word."

"Yes, and here poor Pony has been so sick from it all, and Jim Leonard gets off without anything."

"You are always wanting the tower to fall on the wicked," said Pony's father, laughing. "When it came to the worst, Jim didn't take the melons any more than Pony did. And he seems to have wanted to back out of the whole affair at one time."

"Oh! And do you think that excuses him?"

"No, I don't. But I think he's had a worse time, if that's any comfort, than Pony has. He has suffered the fate of all liars. Sooner or later their lies outwit them and overmaster them, for whenever people believe a liar he is forced to act as if he had spoken the truth. That's worse than having a tower fall on you, or pains in the stomach."

Pony's mother was silent for a moment as if she could not answer, and then she said, "Well, all I know is, I wish there was no such boy in this town as Jim Leonard."

V

ABOUT RUNNING AWAY TO THE INDIAN RESERVATION ON A CANAL-BOAT, AND HOW THE PLAN FAILED

Now, anybody can see the kind of a boy that Jim Leonard was, pretty well; and the strange thing of it was that he could have such a boy as Pony Baker under him so. But, anyway, Pony liked Jim, as much as his mother hated him, and he believed everything Jim said in spite of all that had happened.

After Jim promised to find out whether there was any Indian reservation that you could walk to, he pretended to study out in the geography that the only reservation there was in the State was away up close to Lake Erie, but it was not far from the same canal that ran through the Boy's Town to the lake, and Jim said, "I'll tell you what, Pony! The way to do will be to get into a canal-boat, somehow, and that will take you to the reservation without your hardly having to walk a step; and you can have fun on the boat, too."

Pony agreed that this would be the best way, but he did not really like the notion of living so long among the Indians that he would not remember his father and mother when he saw them; he would like to stay till he was pretty nearly grown up, and then come back in a chief's dress, with eagle plumes all down his back and a bow in his hand, and scare them a little when he first came in the house and then protect them from the tribe and tell them who he was, and enjoy their surprise. But he hated to say this to Jim Leonard, because he would think he was afraid to live with the Indians always. He hardly dared to ask him what the Indians would do to him if they did not adopt him, but he thought he had better, and Jim said:

"Oh, burn you, maybe. But it ain't likely but what they'll adopt you; and if they do they'll take you down to the river, and wash you and scrub you, so's to get all the white man off, and then pull out your hair, a hair at a time, till there's nothing but the scalp-lock left, so that your enemies can scalp you handy; and then you're just as good an Indian as anybody, and nobody can pick on you, or anything. The thing is how to find the canal-boat."

The next morning at school it began to be known that Pony Baker was going to run off on a canal-boat to see the Indians, and all the fellows said how he ought to do it. One of the fellows said that he ought to get to drive the boat horses, and another that he ought to hide on board in the cargo, and come out when the boat was passing the reservation; and another that he ought to go for a cabin-boy on one of the passenger-packets, and then he could get to the Indians twice as soon as he could on a freight-boat. But the trouble was that Pony was so little that they did not believe they would take him either for a driver or a cabin-boy; and he said he was not going to hide in the cargo, because the boats were full of rats, and he was not going to have rats running over him all the time.

Some of the fellows thought this showed a poor spirit in Pony, and wanted him to take his dog along and hunt the rats; they said he could have lots of fun; but others said that

W. D. Howells

the dog would bark as soon as he began to hunt the rats, and then Pony would be found out and put ashore in a minute. The fellows could not think what to do till at last one of them said:

"You know Piccolo Wright?"

"Yes."

"Well, you know his father has got a boat?"

"Yes. Well?"

"Well, and he's got a horse, too; and everything."

"Well, what of it?"

"Get Piccolo to hook the boat and take Pony to the reservation."

The fellows liked this notion so much that they almost hurrahed, and they could hardly wait till school was out and they could go and find Piccolo and ask him whether he would do it. They found him up at the canal basin, where he was fishing off the stern of his father's boat. He was a pretty big boy, though he was not so very old, and he had a lazy, funny face and white hair; and the fellows called him Piccolo because he was learning to play the piccolo flute, and talked about it when he talked at all, but that was not often. He was one of those boys who do not tan or freckle in the sun, but peel, and he always had some loose pieces of fine skin hanging to his nose.

All the fellows came up and began holloing at once, and telling him what they wanted him to do, and he thought it was a first-rate notion, but he kept on fishing, without getting the least bit excited; and he did not say whether he would do it or not, and when the fellows got tired of talking they left him and began to look round the boat. There was a little cabin at one end, and all the rest of the boat was open, and it had been raining, or else the boat had leaked, and it was pretty full of water; and the fellows got down on some loose planks that were floating there, and had fun pushing them up and down, and almost forgot what they had come for. They found a long pump leaning against the side of the boat, with its spout out over the gunwale, and they asked Piccolo if they might pump, and he said they might, and they pumped nearly all the water out after they had got done having fun on the planks.

Some of them went into the cabin and found a little stove there, where Pony could cook his meals, and a bunk where he could sleep, or keep in out of the rain, and they said they wished they were going to run off, too. They took more interest than he did, but they paid him a good deal of attention, and he felt that it was great to be going to run off, and he tried not to be homesick, when he thought of being down there alone at night, and nobody near but Piccolo out on the towpath driving the horse.

The fellows talked it all over, and how they would do. They said that Piccolo ought to hook the boat some Friday night, and the sooner the better, and get a good start before Saturday morning. They were going to start with Pony, and perhaps travel all night with him, and then get off and sleep in the woods, to rest themselves, and then walk home; and the reason that Piccolo ought to hook the boat Friday night was that they could have all Saturday to get back, when there was no school.

If the boat went two miles an hour, which she always did, even if she was loaded with stone from Piccolo's father's

W. D. Howells

quarry, she would be fifteen miles from the Boy's Town by daybreak; and if they kept on travelling night and day, and Pony drove the horse part of the time, they could reach the Indian reservation Monday evening, for they would not want to travel Sunday, because it was against the law, and it was wicked, anyway. If they travelled on Sunday, and a storm came up, just as likely as not the boat would get struck by lightning, and if it did, the lightning would run out along the rope and kill the horse and Piccolo, too, if he was riding. But the way for Piccolo to do was always to come aboard when it began to rain, and that would keep Pony company a little, and they could make the horse go by throwing stones at him.

Pony and Piccolo ought to keep together as much as they could, especially at night, so that if there were robbers, they could defend the boat better. Of course, they could not make the horse go by throwing stones at him in the dark, and the way for them to do was for Pony to get out and ride behind Piccolo. Besides making it safer against robbers, they could keep each other from going to sleep by talking, or else telling stories; or if one of them did doze off, the other could hold him on; and they must take turn about sleeping in the daytime.

But the best way of all to scare the robbers was to have a pistol, and fire it off every little once in a while, so as to let them know that the boat was armed. One of the fellows that had a pistol said he would lend it to Pony if Pony would be sure to send it back from the reservation by Piccolo, for he should want it himself on the Fourth, which was coming in about three weeks. Another fellow that had five cents, which he was saving up till he could get ten, to buy a pack of shooting-crackers, said he would lend it to Pony to buy powder, if he only felt sure that he could get it back to him in time. All the other fellows said he could do it easily, but they did not say how; one of them offered to go and get the powder at once, so as to have it ready.

But Pony told him it would not be of any use, for he had promised his mother that he would not touch a pistol or powder before the Fourth. None of the fellows seemed to think it was strange that he should be willing to run away from home, and yet be so anxious to keep his promise to his mother that he would not use a pistol to defend himself from robbers; and none of them seemed to think it was strange that they should not want Piccolo, if he hooked his father's boat, to travel on Sunday with it.

After a while Piccolo came to the little hatch-door, and looked down into the cabin where the boys were sitting and talking at the tops of their voices; but in about a minute he vanished, very suddenly for him, and they heard him pumping, and then before they knew it, they heard a loud, harsh voice shouting, "Heigh, there!"

They looked round, and at the open window of the cabin on the land-side they saw a man's face, and it seemed to fill the whole window. They knew it must be Piccolo's father, and they just swarmed up the gangway all in a bunch. Some of them fell, but these hung on to the rest, somehow, and they all got to the deck of the cabin together, and began jumping ashore, so that Piccolo's father could not catch them. He was standing on the basin bank, saying something, but they did not know what, and they did not stop to ask, and they began to run every which way.

They all got safely ashore, except Jim Leonard; he fell over the side of the boat between it and the bank, but he scrambled up out of the water like lightning, and ran after the rest. He was pretty long-legged, and he soon caught up, but he was just raining water from his clothes, and it made the fellows laugh so that they could hardly run, to hear him

W. D. Howells

swish when he jolted along. They did not know what to do exactly, till one of them said they ought to go down to the river and go in swimming, and they could wring Jim Leonard's clothes out, and lay them on the shore to dry, and stay in long enough to let them dry. That was what they did, and they ran round through the backs of the gardens and the orchards, and through the alleys, and climbed fences, so that nobody could see them. The day was pretty hot, and by the time they got to the river they were all sweating, so that Jim's clothes were not much damper than the others. He had nothing but a shirt and trousers on, anyway.

After that they did not try to get Piccolo to hook his father's boat, for they said that his father might get after them any time, and he would have a right to do anything he pleased to them, if he caught them. They could not think of any other boat that they could get, and they did not know how Pony could reach the reservation without a canal-boat. That was the reason why they had to give up the notion of his going to the Indians; and if anybody had told them that the Indians were going to come to Pony they would have said he was joking, or else crazy; but this was really what happened. It happened a good while afterwards; so long afterwards that they had about forgotten he ever meant to run off, and they had got done talking about it.

VI

HOW THE INDIANS CAME TO THE BOY'S TOWN AND JIM LEONARD ACTED THE COWARD

Jim Leonard was so mad because he lost his chip-hat in the canal basin, when he fell off the boat (and had to go home bareheaded and tell his mother all about what happened, though his clothes were dry enough, and he might have got off without her noticing anything, if it had not been for his hat) that he would not take any interest in Pony. But he kept on taking an interest in Indians, and he was the most excited fellow in the whole Boy's Town when the Indians came.

The way they came to town was this: The white people around the reservation got tired of having them there, or else they wanted their land, and the government thought it might as well move them out West, where there were more Indians, there were such a very few of them on the reservation; and so it loaded them on three canal-boats and brought them down through the Boy's Town to the Ohio River, and put them on a steamboat, and then took them down to the Mississippi, and put them on a reservation beyond that river.

The boys did not know anything about this, and they would not have cared much if they had. All they knew was that one morning (and it happened to be Saturday) three canal-boats,

W. D. Howells

full of Indians, came into the basin. Nobody ever knew which boy saw them first. It seemed as if all the fellows in the Boy's Town happened to be up at the basin at once, and were standing there when the boats came in. When they saw that they were real Indians, in blankets, with bows and arrows, warriors, squaws, papooses, and everything, they almost went crazy, and when a good many of the Indians came ashore and went over to the court-house yard and began to shoot at quarters and half-dollars that the people stuck into the ground for them to shoot at, the fellows could hardly believe their eyes. They yelled and cheered and tried to get acquainted with the Indian boys, and ran and got their arrows for them, and everything; and if the Indians could only have stayed until the Fourth, which was pretty near now, they would have thought it was the greatest thing that ever happened. Jim Leonard said they belonged to a tribe that had been against the British in the last war, and were the friends of the Long Knives, as they called the Americans. He said that he read it in a book; and he hunted round for Pony Baker, and when he found him he said: "Come here, Pony; I want to tell you something."

Any other time all the other fellows would have crowded around and wanted to know what it was, but now they were so much taken up with the Indians that none of them minded him, and so he got a good chance at Pony alone. Pony was afraid that Jim Leonard wanted him to run off with the Indians, and this was just what he did want.

He said: "You ought to get a blanket and stain your face and hands with walnut juice, and then no one could tell you from the rest of the tribe, and you could go out with them where they're going and hunt buffaloes. It's the greatest chance there ever was. They'll adopt you into the tribe, maybe, as soon as the canal-boats leave, or as quick as they can get to a place where they can pull your hair out and wash you in the canal. I tell you, if I was in your place, I'd do it, Pony."

Pony did not know what to say. He hated to tell Jim Leonard that he had pretty nearly given up the notion of running off for the present, or until his father and mother did something more to make him do it.

Ever since the boys failed so in trying to get Piccolo to hook his father's boat for Pony to run off in, things had been going better with Pony at home. His mother did not stop him from half so many things as she used to do, and lately his father had got to being very good to him: let him lie in bed in the morning, and did not seem to notice when he stayed out with the boys at night, telling stories on the front steps, or playing hide-and-go-whoop, or anything. They seemed to be a great deal taken up with each other and not to mind so much what Pony was doing.

His mother let him go in swimming whenever he asked her, and did not make him promise to keep out of the deep water. She said she would see, when he coaxed her for five cents to get powder for the Fourth, and she let him have one of the boys to spend the night with him once, and she gave them waffles for breakfast. She showed herself something like a mother, and she had told him that if he would be very, very good she would get his father to give him a quarter, so that he could buy two packs of shooting-crackers, as well as five cents' worth of powder for the Fourth. But she put her arms around him and hugged him up to her and kissed his head and said:

"You'll be very careful, Pony, won't you? You're all the little boy we've got, and if anything should happen to you—"

She seemed to be almost crying, and Pony laughed and said: "Why, nothing could happen to you with shooting-crackers";

and she could have the powder to keep for him; and he would just make a snake with it Fourth of July night; put it around through the grass, loose, and then light one end of it, and she would see how it would go off and not make the least noise. But she said she did not want to see it; only he must be careful; and she kissed him again and let him go, and when he got away he could see her wiping her eyes. It seemed to him that she was crying a good deal in those days, and he could not understand what it was about. She was scared at any little thing, and would whoop at the least noise, and when his father would say: "Lucy, my dear girl!" she would burst out crying and say that she could not help it. But she got better and better to Pony all the time, and it was this that now made him ashamed with Jim Leonard, because it made him not want to run off so much.

He dug his toe into the turf in the court-house yard under the locust-tree, and did not say anything till Jim Leonard asked him if he was afraid to go off and live with the Indians, because if he was going to be a cowardy-calf like that, it was all that Jim Leonard wanted to do with him.

Pony denied that he was afraid, but he said that he did not know how to talk Indian, and he did not see how he was going to get along without.

Jim Leonard laughed and said if that was all, he need not be anxious. "The Indians don't talk at all, hardly, even among each other. They just make signs; didn't you know that? If you want something to eat you point to your mouth and chew; and if you want a drink, you open your mouth and keep swallowing. When you want to go to sleep you shut your eyes and lean your cheek over on your hand, this way. That's all the signs you need to begin with, and you'll soon learn the rest. Now, say, are you going with the Indians, or ain't you going? It's your only chance. Why, Pony, what are you afraid of? Hain't you always wanted to sleep out-doors and not do anything but hunt?"

Pony had to confess that he had, and then Jim Leonard said: "Well, then, that's what you'll do if you go with the Indians. I suppose you'll have to go on the warpath with them when you get out there; and if it's against the whites you won't like it at first; but you've got to remember what the whites have done to the Indians ever since they discovered America, and you'll soon get to feeling like an Indian anyway. One thing is, you've got to get over being afraid."

That made Pony mad, and he said: "I ain't afraid now."

"I know that," said Jim Leonard. "But what I mean is, that if you get hurt you mustn't hollo, or cry, or anything; and even when they're scalping you, you mustn't even make a face, so as to let them know that you feel it."

By this time some of the other fellows began to come around to hear what Jim Leonard was saying to Pony. A good many of the Indians had gone off anyway, for the people had stopped sticking quarters into the ground for them to shoot at, and they could not shoot at nothing. Jim Leonard saw the fellows crowding around, but he went on as if he did not notice them. "You've got to go without eating anything for weeks when the medicine-man tells you to; and when you come back from the warpath, and they have a scalp-dance, you've got to keep dancing till you drop in a fit. When they give a dog feast you must eat dog stew until you can't swallow another mouthful, and you'll be so full that you'll just have to lay around for days without moving. But the great thing is to bear any kind of pain without budging or saying a single word. Maybe you're used to holloing now when you get hurt?"

Pony confessed that he holloed a little; the others tried to look as if they never holloed at all, and Jim Leonard went on:

"Well, you've got to stop that. If an arrow was to go through you and stick out at your back, or anywhere, you must just reach around and pull it out and not speak. When you're having the sun-dance—I think it's the sun-dance, but I ain't really certain—you have to stick a hook through you, right here"—he grabbed Pony by the muscles on his shoulders—"and let them pull you up on a pole and hang there as long as they please. They'll let you practise gradually so that you won't mind hardly anything. Why, I've practised a good deal by myself, and now I've got so that I believe if you was to stick me with—"

All of a sudden something whizzed along the ground and Jim Leonard stooped over and caught one of his feet up in his hand, and began to cry and to hollo: "Oh, oh, oh! Ow, ow, ow! Oh, my foot! Oh, it's broken; I know it is! Oh, run for the doctor, do, Pony Baker! I know I'm going to die! Oh, dear, oh dear, oh dear!"

All the boys came crowding around to see what the matter was, and the men came, too, and pretty soon some one found an arrow in the grass, and then they knew that it was a stray arrow that had hit Jim Leonard on the side of the foot, after missing one of the dimes that was stuck in the ground. It was blunt, and it had not hurt him that anybody could see, except rubbed the skin off a little on the ankle-bone. But Jim Leonard began to limp away towards home, and now, as the Indians had all gone back to their boats, and the fellows had nothing else to do, they went along with him.

Archy Hawkins held him up on one side, and Hen Billard on the other, and Archy said, "I tell you, when I heard Jim yell, I thought it was a real Indian," and Hen said:

"I thought it was the scalp-halloo."

Archy said, "The way I came to think it was a real Indian was that a real Indian never makes any noise when he's hurt," and Hen said:

"I thought it was the scalp-halloo, because Jim was stooping over as if he was tearing the scalp off of a white man. He's been practising, you know."

"Well, practice makes perfect. I reckon if Jim hasn't got so far that he would smile when you scalped him, or just laugh if you shot an arrow through him, or would let you stick a hook into him, and pull him up to the top of a pole, it's because he's begun at the other end. I'll bet he could eat himself full of dog stew, and lay around three days without stirring."

Jim Leonard thought the fellows had come along to pity him and help him; but when he heard Archy Hawkins say that, and Hen Billard began to splutter and choke with the laugh he was holding in, he flung them off and began to fight at them with his fists, and strike right and left blindly. He broke out crying, and then the fellows made a ring around him and danced and mocked him.

"Hey, Jim, what'd you do if they pulled your hair out?"

"Jimmy, oh, Jim! Would you hollo much louder if they tomahawked you?"

"Show your uncle how to dance till you drop, Jim."

They kept on till Jim Leonard picked up stones to stone them, and then they all ran away, jumping and jeering till they got out of sight. It was about dinner-time, anyway.

No one was left but Pony Baker. He stooped down over Jim when he sat crying over his foot. "Does it hurt you much, Jimmy?" he asked.

"Yes, it hurts dreadfully, Pony. The skin's all rubbed off. I'm afraid it's broken my leg."

"Well, let me help you home," said Pony. "Your mother can tie it up, then."

He made Jim lean on him, and keep trying his foot, and pretty soon they found he could walk with it nearly the same as the other foot, and before they got to Jim's house they were talking and laughing together.

After that, Pony Baker gave up running off to the Indians. He about gave up running off altogether. He had a splendid Fourth of July. His mother would not let him stay up the whole of the night before, but she let him get up at four o'clock, and fire off both his packs of shooting-crackers; and though she had forbidden him to go down to the river-bank where the men were firing off the cannon, he hardly missed it. He felt sleepy as soon as his crackers were done, and another fellow who was with him came into the parlor, and they both lay down on the carpet and went to sleep there, and slept till breakfast-time. After breakfast he went up to the court-house yard, with some other fellows, and then, after dinner, when they all came round and begged, and the big fellows promised to watch out for Pony, his mother let him go out to the second lock with them, and go in swimming in the canal. He did not know why this should be such a great privilege, but it was. He had never been out to the second lock before. It was outside of the corporation line, and that was a great thing in itself.

After supper, Pony's mother let him fire off his powder-snake, and she even came out and looked at it, with her fingers in her ears. He promised her that it wouldn't make any noise, but she could not believe him; and when the flash came, she gave a little whoop, and ran in-doors. It shamed him before the boys, for fear they would laugh; and she acted even worse when his father wished to let him go up to the court-house yard to see the fireworks.

A lot of the fellows were going, and he was to go with the crowd, but his father was to come a little behind, so as to see that nothing happened to him; and when they were just starting off what should she do but hollo to his father from the door where she was standing, "Do be careful of the child, Henry!" It did not seem as if she could be a good mother when she tried, and she was about the afraidest mother in the Boy's Town.

All the way up to the court-house the boys kept snickering and whispering, "Don't stump your toe, child," and "Be careful of the child, boys," and things like that till Pony had to fight some of them. Then they stopped. They were afraid his father would hear, anyway.

But the fireworks were splendid, and the fellows were very good to Pony, because his father stood in the middle of the crowd and treated them to lemonade, and they did not plague, any more, going home. It was ten o'clock when Pony got home; it was the latest he had ever been up.

The very Fourth of July before that one he had been up pretty nearly as late listening to his cousin, Frank Baker, telling about the fun he had been having at a place called Pawpaw Bottom; and the strange thing that happened there, if it did happen, for nobody could exactly find out. So I think I had better break off again from Pony, and say what it was that Frank told; and after that I can go on with Pony's running off.

VII

HOW FRANK BAKER SPENT THE FOURTH AT PAWPAW BOTTOM, AND SAW THE FOURTH OF JULY BOY

It was the morning of the Fourth, and Frank was so anxious to get through with his wood-sawing, and begin celebrating with the rest of the boys, that he hardly knew what to do. He had a levvy (as the old Spanish *real* used to be called in southern Ohio) in his pocket, and he was going to buy a pack of shooting-crackers for ten cents, and spend the other two cents for powder. He had no pistol, but he knew a fellow that would lend him his pistol part of the time, and he expected to have about the best Fourth he ever had. He had been up since three o'clock watching the men fire the old six-pounder on the river-bank; and he was going to get his mother to let him go up to the fireworks in the court-house yard after dark.

But now it did not seem as if he could get wood enough sawed. Twice he asked his mother if she thought he had enough, but she said "Not near," and just as Jake Milrace rode up the saw caught in a splinter of the tough oak log Frank was sawing and bumped back against Frank's nose; and he would have cried if it had not been for what Jake began to say.

He said he was going to Pawpaw Bottom to spend the Fourth at a fellow's named Dave Black, and he told Frank he ought to go too; for there were plenty of mulberries on Dave's father's farm, and the early apples were getting ripe enough to eat, if you pounded them on a rock; and you could go in swimming, and everything. Jake said there was the greatest swimming-hole at Pawpaw Bottom you ever saw, and they had a log in the water there that you could have lots of fun with. Frank ran into the house to ask his mother if he might go, and he hardly knew what to do when she asked him if there was wood enough yet to get dinner and supper. But his Aunt Manda was spending the summer with his mother, and she said she reckoned she could pick up chips to do all the cooking they needed, such a hot day; and Frank ran out to the cow-house, where they kept the pony, because the Bakers had no stable, and saddled him, and was off with Jake Milrace in about a minute.

The pony was short and fat and lazy, and he had to be whipped to make him keep up with Jake's horse. It was not exactly Jake's horse; it was his sister's husband's horse, and he had let Jake have it because he would not be using it himself on the Fourth of July. It was tall and lean, and it held its head so high up that it was no use to pull on the bridle when it began to jump and turn round and round, which it did every time Frank whipped his pony to keep even with Jake. It would shy and sidle, and dart so far ahead that the pony would get discouraged and would lag back, and have to be whipped up again; and then the whole thing would have to be gone through with the same as at first. The boys did not have much chance to talk, but they had a splendid time riding along, and when they came to a cool, dark place in the woods they pretended there were Indians; and at the same time they kept a sharp eye out for squirrels. If they had seen any, and had a gun with them, they could have shot one easily, for squirrels are not afraid of you when you are on horseback; and, as it was, Jake Milrace came pretty near killing a quail that they saw in the road by a wheat-field. He dropped his bridle and took aim with his forefinger, and pulled back his thumb like a trigger; and if his horse had not jumped, and his finger had been loaded, he would surely have killed the quail, it was so close to him. They could hear the bob-whites whistling all through the stubble and among the shocks of wheat.

Jake did not know just where Dave Black's farm was, but after a while they came to a blacksmith's shop, and the blacksmith told them to take a lane that they would come to on the left, and then go through a piece of woods and across a field till they came to a creek; then ford the creek and keep straight on, and they would be in sight of the house. It did not seem strange to Frank that they should be going to visit a boy without knowing where he lived, but afterwards he was not surprised when Dave Black's folks did not appear to expect them. They kept on, and did as the blacksmith told them, and soon enough they got to a two-story log-cabin, with a man in front of it working at a wheat-fan, for it was nearly time to thresh the wheat. The man said he was Dave Black's father; he did not act as if he was very glad to see them, but he told them to put their horses in the barn, and he said that Dave was out in the pasture hauling rails.

Frank thought that was a queer way of spending the Fourth of July, but he did not say anything, and on their way out to the pasture Jake explained that Dave's father was British, and did not believe much in the Fourth of July, anyway. They found Dave easily enough, and he answered Jake's "Hello!" with another when the boys came up. He had a two-horse wagon, and he was loading it with rails from a big pile; there were two dogs with him, and when they saw the boys they came towards them snarling and ruffling the hair on their backs. Jake said not to mind them—they would not bite; but they snuffed so close to Frank's bare legs that he wished Dave would call them off. They slunk away, though, when they heard him speak to the boys; and then Jake Milrace told Dave Black who Frank was, and they began to feel acquainted, especially when Jake said they had come to spend the Fourth of July with Dave.

He said, "First rate," and he explained that he had his foot tied up the way they saw because he had a stone-bruise which he had got the first day he began to go barefoot in the spring; but now it was better. He said there was a bully swimming-hole in the creek, and he would show them where it was as soon as he had got done hauling his rails. The boys took that for a kind of hint, and they pulled off their roundabouts and set to work with him.

Frank thought it was not exactly like the Fourth, but he did not say anything, and they kept loading up the rails and hauling them to the edge of the field where Dave's father was going to build the fence, and then unloading them, and going back to the pile for more. It seemed to Frank that there were about a thousand rails in that pile, and they were pretty heavy ones—oak and hickory and walnut—and you had to be careful how you handled them, or you would get your hands stuck full of splinters. He wondered what Jake Milrace was thinking, and whether it was the kind of Fourth he had expected to have; but Jake did not say anything, and he hated to ask him. Sometimes it appeared to Frank that sawing wood was nothing to it; but they kept on loading rails, and unloading them in piles about ten feet apart, where they were wanted; and then going back to the big pile for more. They worked away in the blazing sun till the sweat poured off their faces, and Frank kept thinking what a splendid time the fellows were having with pistols and shooting-crackers up in the Boy's Town; but still he did not say anything, and pretty soon he had his reward. When they got half down through

W. D. Howells

the rail-pile they came to a bumblebees' nest, which the dogs thought was a rat-hole at first. One of them poked his nose into it, but he pulled it out quicker than wink and ran off howling and pawing his face and rubbing his head in the ground or against the boys' legs. Even when the dogs found out that it was not rats they did not show any sense. As soon as they rubbed a bee off they would come yelping and howling back for more; and hopping round and barking; and then when they got another bee, or maybe a half-dozen (for the bees did not always fight fair), they would streak off again and jump into the air, and roll on the ground till the boys almost killed themselves laughing.

The boys went into the woods, and got pawpaw branches, and came back and fought the bumblebees till they drove them off. It was just like the battle of Bunker Hill; but Frank did not say so, because Dave's father was British, till Dave said it himself, and then they all pretended the bees were Mexicans; it was just a little while after the Mexican War. When they drove the bees off, they dug their nest out; it was beautifully built in regular cells of gray paper, and there was a little honey in it; about a spoonful for each boy.

Frank was glad that he had not let out his disappointment with the kind of Fourth they were having; and just then the horn sounded from the house for dinner, and the boys all got into the wagon, and rattled off to the barn. They put out the horses and fed them, and as soon as they could wash themselves at the rain-barrel behind the house, they went in and sat down with the family at dinner. It was a farmer's dinner, as it used to be in southern Ohio fifty years ago: a deep dish of fried salt pork swimming in its own fat, plenty of shortened biscuit and warm green-apple sauce, with good butter. The Boy's Town boys did not like the looks of the fat pork, but they were wolf-hungry, and the biscuit were splendid. In the middle of the table there was a big crock of buttermilk, all cold and dripping from the spring-house where it had been standing in the running water; then there was a hot apple-pie right out of the oven; and they made a pretty fair meal, after all.

After dinner they hauled more rails, and when they had hauled all the rails there were, they started for the swimming-hole in the creek. On the way they came to a mulberry-tree in the edge of the woods-pasture, and it was so full of berries and they were so ripe that the grass which the cattle had cropped short was fairly red under the tree. The boys got up into the tree and gorged themselves among the yellow-hammers and woodpeckers; and Frank and Jake kept holloing out to each other how glad they were they had come; but Dave kept quiet, and told them to wait till they came to the swimming-hole.

It was while they were in the tree that something happened which happened four times in all that day, if it really happened: nobody could say afterwards whether it had or not. Frank was reaching out for a place in the tree where the berries seemed thicker than anywhere else, when a strong blaze of light flashed into his eyes, and blinded him.

"Oh, hello, Dave Black!" he holloed. "That's mean! What are you throwin' that light in my face for?"

But he laughed at the joke, and he laughed more when Dave shouted back, "I ain't throwin' no light in your face."

"Yes, you are; you've got a piece of look-in'-glass, and you're flashin' it in my face."

"Wish I may die, if I have," said Dave, so seriously that Frank had to believe him.

"Well, then, Jake Milrace has."

"I hain't, any such thing," said Jake, and then Dave Black roared back, laughing: "Oh, I'll tell you! It's one of the pieces of tin we strung along that line in the corn-field to keep the crows off, corn-plantin' time."

The boys shouted together at the joke on Frank, and Dave parted the branches for a better look at the corn-field.

"Well, well! Heigh there!" he called towards the field. "Oh, he's gone now!" he said to the other boys, craning their necks out to see, too. "But he *was* doing it, Frank. If I could ketch that feller!"

"Somebody you know? Let's get him to come along," said Jake and Frank, one after the other.

"I couldn't tell," said Dave. "He slipped into the woods when he heard me holler. If it's anybody I know, he'll come out again. Don't seem to notice him; that's the best way."

For a while, though, they stopped to look, now and then; but no more flashes came from the corn-field, and the boys went on cramming themselves with berries; they all said they had got to stop, but they went on till Dave said: "I don't believe it's going to do us any good to go in swimming if we eat too many of these mulberries. I reckon we better quit, now."

The others said they reckoned so, too, and they all got down from the tree, and started for the swimming-hole. They had to go through a piece of woods to get to it, and in the shadow of the trees they did not notice that a storm was coming up till they heard it thunder. By that time they were on the edge of the woods, and there came a flash of lightning and a loud thunder-clap, and the rain began to fall in big drops. The boys saw a barn in the field they had reached, and they ran for it; and they had just got into it when the rain came down with all its might. Suddenly Jake said: "I'll tell you what! Let's take off our clothes and have a shower-bath!" And in less than a minute they had their clothes off, and were out in the full pour, dancing up and down, and yelling like Indians. That made them think of playing Indians, and they pretended the barn was a settler's cabin, and they were stealing up on it through the tall shocks of wheat. They captured it easily, and they said if the lightning would only strike it and set it on fire so it would seem as if the Indians had done it, it would be great; but the storm was going round, and they had to be satisfied with being settlers, turn about, and getting scalped.

It was easy to scalp Frank, because he wore his hair long, as the town boys liked to do in those days, but Jake lived with his sister, and he had to do as she said. She said a boy had no business with long hair; and she had lately cropped his close to his skull. Dave's father cut his hair round the edges of a bowl, which he had put on Dave's head for a pattern; the other boys could get a pretty good grip of it, if they caught it on top, where the scalp-lock belongs; but Dave would duck and dodge so that they could hardly get their hands on it. All at once they heard him call out from around the corner of the barn, where he had gone to steal up on them, when it was their turn to be settlers: "Aw, now, Jake Milrace, that ain't fair! I'm an Indian, now. You let go my hair."

"Who's touchin' your old hair?" Jake shouted back, from the inside of the barn. "You must be crazy. Hurry up, if you're ever goin' to attack us. I want to get out in the rain, myself, awhile."

Frank was outside, pretending to be at work in the field, and waiting for the Indians to creep on him, and when Jake shouted for Dave to hurry, he looked over his shoulder and saw a white figure, naked like his own, flit round the left-hand corner of the barn. Then he had to stoop over, so that Dave could tomahawk him easily, and he did not see anything more, but Jake yelled from the barn: "Oh, you got that fellow with you, have you? Then he's got to be settler next time. Come on, now. Oh, do hurry up!"

Frank raised his head to see the other boy, but there was only Dave Black, coming round the right-hand corner of the barn.

"You're crazy yourself, Jake. There ain't nobody here but me and Frank."

"There is, too!" Jake retorted. "Or there was, half a second ago."

But Dave was busy stealing on Frank, who was bending over, pretending to hoe, and after he had tomahawked Frank, he gave the scalp-halloo, and Jake came running out of the barn, and had to be chased round it twice, so that he could fall breathless on his own threshold, and be scalped in full sight of his family. Then Dave pretended to be a war-party of Wyandots, and he gathered up sticks, and pretended to set the barn on fire. By this time Frank and Jake had come to life, and were Wyandots, too, and they all joined hands and danced in front of the barn.

"There! There he is again!" shouted Jake. "Who's crazy *now*, I should like to know?"

"Where? Where?" yelled both the other boys.

"There! Right in the barn door. Or he *was*, quarter of a second ago," said Jake, and they all dropped one another's hands, and rushed into the barn and began to search it.

They could not find anybody, and Dave Black said: "Well, he's the quickest feller! Must 'a' got up into the mow, and jumped out of the window, and broke for the woods while we was lookin' down here. But if I get my hands onto him, oncet!"

They all talked and shouted and quarrelled and laughed at once; but they had to give the other fellow up; he had got away for that time, and they ran out into the rain again to let it wash off the dust and chaff, which they had got all over them in their search. The rain felt so good and cool that they stood still and took it without playing any more, and talked quietly. Dave decided that the fellow who had given them the slip was a new boy whose folks had come into the neighborhood since school had let out in the spring, so that he had not got acquainted yet; but Dave allowed that he would teach him a few tricks as good as his own when he got at him.

The storm left a solid bank of clouds in the east for a while after it was all blue in the western half of the sky, and a rainbow came out against the clouds. It looked so firm and thick that Dave said you could cut it with a scythe. It seemed to come solidly down to the ground in the woods in front of the hay-mow window, and the boys said it would be easy to get the crock of gold at the end of it if they were only in the woods. "I'll bet that feller's helpin' himself," said Dave, and they began to wonder how many dollars a crock of gold was worth, anyhow; they decided about a million. Then they wondered how much of a crock full of gold a boy could get into his pockets; and they all laughed when Jake said he reckoned it would depend upon the size of the crock. "I don't believe that fellow could carry much of it away if he hain't got more on than he had in front of the barn." That put Frank in mind of the puzzle about the three men that found a treasure in the road when they were travelling together: the blind man saw it, and the man without arms picked it up, and

W. D. Howells

the naked man put it in his pocket. It was the first time Dave had heard the puzzle, and he asked, "Well, what's the answer?" But before Frank could tell him, Jake started up and pointed to the end of the rainbow, where it seemed to go into the ground against the woods.

"Oh! look! look!" he panted out, and they all looked, but no one could see anything except Jake. It made him mad. "Why, you must be blind!" he shouted, and he kept pointing. "Don't you see him? There, there! Oh, now, the rainbow's going out, and you can't see him any more. He's gone into the woods again. Well, I don't know what your eyes are good for, anyway."

He tried to tell them what he had seen; he could only make out that it must be the same boy, but now he had his clothes on: white linen pantaloons and roundabout, like what you had on May day, or the Fourth if you were going to the Sunday-school picnic. Dave wanted him to tell what he looked like, but Jake could not say anything except that he was very smiling-looking, and seemed as if he would like to be with him; Jake said he was just going to hollo for him to come over when the rainbow began to go out; and then the fellow slipped back into the woods; it was more like melting into the woods.

"And how far off do you think you could see a boy smile?" Dave asked, scornfully.

"How far off can you say a rainbow is?" Jake retorted.

"I can say how far off that piece of woods is," said Dave, with a laugh. He got to his feet, and began to pull at the other boys, to make them get up. "Come along, if you're ever goin' to the swimmin'-hole."

The sun was bright and hot, and the boys left the barn, and took across the field to the creek. The storm must have been very heavy, for the creek was rushing along bank-full, and there was no sign left of Dave's swimming-hole. But they had had such a glorious shower-bath that they did not want to go in swimming, anyway, and they stood and watched the yellow water pouring over the edge of a mill-dam that was there, till Dave happened to think of building a raft and going out on the dam. Jake said, "First rate!" and they all rushed up to a place where there were some boards on the bank; and they got pieces of old rope at the mill, and tied the boards together, till they had a good raft, big enough to hold them, and then they pushed it into the water and got on it. They said they were on the Ohio River, and going from Cincinnati to Louisville. Dave had a long pole to push with, like the boatmen on the keel-boats in the early times, and Jake had a board to steer with; Frank had another board to paddle with, on the other side of the raft from Dave; and so they set on their journey.

The dam was a wide, smooth sheet of water, with trees growing round the edge, and some of them hanging so low over it that they almost touched it. The boys made trips back and forth across the dam, and to and from the edge of the fall, till they got tired of it, and they were wanting something to happen, when Dave stuck his pole deep into the muddy bottom, and set his shoulder hard against the top of the pole, with a "Here she goes, boys, over the Falls of the Ohio!" and he ran along the edge of the raft from one end to the other.

Frank and Dave had both straightened up to watch him. At the stern of the raft Dave tried to pull up his pole for another good push, but it stuck fast in the mud at the bottom of the dam, and before Dave knew what he was about, the raft shot from under his feet, and he went overboard with his pole in his hand, as if he were taking a flying leap with it. The next

W. D. Howells

minute he dropped into the water heels first, and went down out of sight. He came up blowing water from his mouth, and holloing and laughing, and took after the raft, where the other fellows were jumping up and down, and bending back and forth, and screaming and yelling at the way he looked hurrying after his pole, and then dangling in the air, and now showing his black head in the water like a musk-rat swimming for its hole. They were having such a good time mocking him that they did not notice how his push had sent the raft swiftly in under the trees by the shore, and the first thing they knew, one of the low branches caught them, and scraped them both off the raft into the water, almost on top of Dave. Then it was Dave's turn to laugh, and he began: "What's the matter, boys? Want to help find the other end of that pole?"

Jake was not under the water any longer than Dave had been, but Frank did not come up so soon. They looked among the brush by the shore, to see if he was hiding there and fooling them, but they could not find him. "He's stuck in some snag at the bottom," said Dave; "we got to dive for him"; but just then Frank came up, and swam feebly for the shore. He crawled out of the water, and after he got his breath, he said, "I got caught, down there, in the top of an old tree."

"Didn't I tell you so?" Dave shouted into Jake's ear.

"Why, Jake was there till I got loose," said Frank, looking stupidly at him.

"No, I wasn't," said Jake. "I was up long ago, and I was just goin' to dive for you; so was Dave."

"Then it was that other fellow," said Frank. "I thought it didn't look overmuch like Jake, anyway."

"Oh, pshaw!" Dave jeered. "How could you tell, in that muddy water?"

"I don't know," Frank answered. "It was all light round him. Looked like he had a piece of the rainbow on him, or foxfire."

"I reckon if I find him," said Dave, "I'll take his piece of rainbow off'n him pretty quick. That's the fourth time that feller's fooled us to-day. Where d'you s'pose he came up? Oh, *I* know! He got out on the other side under them trees, while we was huntin' for Frank, and not noticin'. How'd he look, anyway?"

"I don't know; I just saw him half a second. Kind of smiling, and like he wanted to play."

"Well, I know him," said Dave. "It's the new boy, and the next time I see him—Oh, hello! There goes our raft!"

It was drifting slowly down towards the edge of the dam, and the boys all three plunged into the water again, and swam out to it, and climbed up on it.

They had the greatest kind of a time, and when they had played castaway sailors, Frank and Jake wanted to send the raft over the edge of the dam; but Dave said it might get into the head-race of the mill and tangle itself up in the wheel, and spoil the wheel.

So they took the raft apart and carried the boards on shore, and then tried to think what they would do next. The first thing was to take off their clothes and see about drying them. But they had no patience for that; and so they wrung them out as dry as they could and put them on again; they had left their roundabouts at Dave's house, anyway, and so had

W. D. Howells

nothing on but a shirt and trousers apiece. The sun was out hot after the rain, and their clothes were almost dry by the time they got to Dave's house. They went with him to the woods-pasture on the way, and helped him drive home the cows, and they wanted him to get his mother to make his father let him go up to the Boy's Town with them and see the fireworks; but he said it would be no use; and then they understood that if a man was British, of course he would not want his boy to celebrate the Fourth of July by going to the fireworks. They felt sorry for Dave, but they both told him that they had had more fun than they ever had in their lives before, and they were coming the next Fourth and going to bring their guns with them. Then they could shoot quails or squirrels, if they saw any, and the firing would celebrate the Fourth at the same time, and his father could not find any fault.

It seemed to Frank that it was awful to have a father that was British; but when they got to Dave's house, and his father asked them how they had spent the afternoon, he did not seem to be so very bad. He asked them whether they had got caught in the storm, and if that was what made their clothes wet, and when they told him what had happened, he sat down on the wood-pile and laughed till he shook all over.

Then Frank and Jake thought they had better be going home, but Dave's mother would not let them start without something to eat; and she cut them each a slice of bread the whole width and length of the loaf, and spread the slices with butter, and then apple-butter, and then brown sugar. The boys thought they were not hungry, but when they began to eat they found out that they were, and before they knew it they had eaten the slices all up. Dave's mother said they must come and see Dave again some time, and she acted real clever; she was an American, anyway.

They got their horses and started home. It was almost sundown now, and they heard the turtle-doves cooing in the woods, and the bob-whites whistling from the stubble, and there were so many squirrels among the trees in the woods-pastures, and on the fences, that Frank could hardly get Jake along; and if it had not been for Jake's horse, that ran whenever Frank whipped up his pony, they would not have got home till dark. They smelt ham frying in some of the houses they passed, and that made them awfully hungry; one place there was coffee, too.

When they reached Frank's house he found that his mother had kept supper hot for him, and she came out and said Jake must come in with him, if his family would not be uneasy about him; and Jake said he did not believe they would. He tied his horse to the outside of the cow-house, and he came in, and Frank's mother gave them as much baked chicken as they could hold, with hot bread to sop in the gravy; and she had kept some coffee hot for Frank, so that they made another good meal. They told her what a bully time they had had, and how they had fallen into the dam; but she did not seem to think it was funny; she said it was a good thing they were not all drowned, and she believed they had taken their deaths of cold, anyway. Frank was afraid she was going to make him go up stairs and change his clothes, when he heard the boys begin to sound their call of "Ee-o-wee" at the front door, and he and Jake snatched their hats and ran out. There was a lot of boys at the gate; Hen Billard was there, and Archy Hawkins and Jim Leonard; there were some little fellows, and Frank's cousin Pony was there; he said his mother had said he might stay till his father came for him.

Hen Billard had his thumb tied up from firing too big a load out of his brass pistol. The pistol burst, and the barrel was all curled back like a dandelion stem in water; he had it in his pocket to show. Archy Hawkins's face was full of little blue

W. D. Howells

specks from pouring powder on a coal and getting it flashed up into his face when he was blowing the coal; some of his eye-winkers were singed off. Jim Leonard had a rag round his hand, and he said a whole pack of shooting-crackers had gone off in it before he could throw them away, and burned the skin off; the fellows dared him to let them see it, but he would not; and then they mocked him. They all said there had never been such a Fourth of July in the Boy's Town before; and Frank and Jake let them brag as much as they wanted to, and when the fellows got tired, and asked them what they had done at Pawpaw Bottom, and they said, "Oh, nothing much; just helped Dave Black haul rails," they set up a jeer that you could hear a mile.

Then Jake said, as if he just happened to think of it, "And fought bumblebees."

And Frank put in, "And took a shower-bath in the thunder-storm."

And Jake said, "And eat mulberries."

And Frank put in again, "And built a raft."

And Jake said, "And Dave got pulled into the mill-dam."

And Frank wound up, "And Jake and I got swept overboard."

By that time the fellows began to feel pretty small, and they crowded round and wanted to hear every word about it. Then Jake and Frank tantalized them, and said of course it was no Fourth at all, it was only just fun, till the fellows could not stand it any longer, and then Frank jumped up from where he was sitting on his front steps, and holloed out, "I'll show you how Dave looked when his pole pulled him in," and he acted it all out about Dave's pole pulling him into the water.

Jake waited till he was done, and then he jumped up and said, "I'll show you how Frank and me looked when we got swept overboard," and he acted it out about the limb of the tree scraping them off the raft while they were laughing at Dave and not noticing.

As soon as they got the boys to yelling, Jake and Frank both showed how they fought the bumblebees, and how the dogs got stung, and ran round trying to rub the bees off against the ground, and your legs, and everything, till the boys fell down and rolled over, it made them laugh so. Jake and Frank showed how they ran out into the rain from the barn, and stood in it, and told how good and cool it felt; and they told about sitting up in the mulberry-tree, and how twenty boys could not have made the least hole in the berries. They told about the quails and the squirrels; and they showed how Frank had to keep whipping up his pony, and how Jake's horse kept wheeling and running away; and some of the fellows said they were going with them the next Fourth.

Hen Billard tried to turn it off, and said: "Pshaw! You can have that kind of a Fourth any day in the country. Who's going up to the court-house yard to see the fireworks?"

He and Archy Hawkins and the big boys ran off, whooping, and the little fellows felt awfully, because their mothers had said they must not go. Just then, Pony Baker's father came for him, and he said he guessed they could see the fireworks from Frank's front steps; and Jake stayed with Frank, and Frank's father came out, and his aunt and mother leaned out of the window, and watched, while the Roman candles shot up, and the rockets climbed among the stars.

They were all so much taken up in watching that they did not notice one of the neighbor women who had come over from her house and joined them, till Mrs. Baker happened to see

W. D. Howells

her, and called out: "Why, Mrs. Fogle, where did you spring from? Do come in here with Manda and me. I didn't see you, in your black dress."

"No, I'm going right back," said Mrs. Fogle. "I just come over a minute to see the fireworks—for Wilford; you can't see them from my side."

"Oh," said Mrs. Baker, softly. "Well, I'm real glad you came. You ought to have heard the boys, here, telling about the kind of Fourth they had at Pawpaw Bottom. I don't know when I've laughed so much."

"Well, I reckon it's just as well I wasn't here. I couldn't have helped in the laughing much. It seems pretty hard my Wilford couldn't been having a good time with the rest to-day. He was always such a Fourth-of-July boy."

"But he's happy where he is, Mrs. Fogle," said Mrs. Baker, gently.

"Well, I know he'd give anything to been here with the boys to-day—I don't care where he is. And he's been here, too; I just know he has; I've felt him, all day long, teasing at me to let him go off with your Frank and Jake, here; he just fairly loved to be with them, and he never done any harm. Oh, my, my! I don't see how I used to deny him."

She put up her apron to her face, and ran sobbing across the street again to her own house; they heard the door close after her in the dark.

"I declare," said Mrs. Baker, "I've got half a mind to go over to her."

"Better not," said Pony Baker's father.

"Well, I reckon you're right, Henry," Mrs. Baker assented.

They did not talk gayly any more; when the last rocket had climbed the sky, Jake Milrace rose and said in a whisper he must be going.

After he was gone, Frank told, as if he had just thought of it, about the boy that had fooled them so, at Pawpaw Bottom; and he was surprised at the way his mother and his Uncle Henry questioned him up about it.

"Well, now," she said, "I'm glad poor Mrs. Fogle wasn't here, or—" She stopped, and her brother-in-law rose, with the hand of his sleepy little son in his own.

"I think Pony had better say good-night now, while he can. Frank, you've had a remarkable Fourth. Good-night, all. I wish I had spent the day at Pawpaw Bottom myself."

Before they slept that night, Pony's mother said: "Well, I'd just as soon you'd kept that story to yourself till morning, Henry. I shall keep thinking about it, and not sleep a wink. How in the world do you account for it?"

"I don't account for it," said Pony's father.

"Now, that won't do! What do you think?"

"Well, if it was *one* boy that saw the fourth boy it might be a simple case of lying."

"Frank Baker never told a lie in his life. He couldn't."

"Perhaps Jake could, or Dave. But as they all three saw the boy at different times, why, it's—"

W. D. Howells

"What?"

"It's another thing."

"Now, you can't get out of it that way, Henry. Do you believe that the child longed so to be back here that—"

"Ah, who knows? There's something very strange about all
that. But we can't find our way out, except by the short-cut of
supposing that nothing of the kind happened."

"You can't suppose that, though, if all three of the boys say it
did."

"I can suppose that they think it happened, or made each
other think so."

Pony's mother drew a long sigh. "Well, I know what *I* shall
always think," she said.

VIII

HOW PONY BAKER CAME PRETTY NEAR
RUNNING OFF WITH A CIRCUS

Just before the circus came, about the end of July, something happened that made Pony mean to run off more than anything that ever was. His father and mother were coming home from a walk, in the evening; it was so hot nobody could stay in the house, and just as they were coming to the front steps Pony stole up behind them and tossed a snowball which he had got out of the garden at his mother, just for fun. The flower struck her very softly on her hair, for she had no bonnet on, and she gave a jump and a hollo that made Pony laugh; and then she caught him by the arm and boxed his ears.

"Oh, my goodness! It was you, was it, you good-for-nothing boy? I thought it was a bat!" she said, and she broke out crying and ran into the house, and would not mind his father, who was calling after her, "Lucy, Lucy, my dear child!"

Pony was crying, too, for he did not intend to frighten his mother, and when she took his fun as if he had done something wicked he did not know what to think. He stole off to bed and he lay there crying in the dark and expecting that she would come to him, as she always did, to have him

W. D. Howells

say that he was sorry when he had been wicked, or to tell him that she was sorry, when she thought she had not been quite fair with him. But she did not come, and after a good while his father came and said: "Are you awake, Pony? I am sorry your mother misunderstood your fun. But you mustn't mind it, dear boy. She's not well, and she's very nervous."

"I don't care!" Pony sobbed out. "She won't have a chance to touch me again!" For he had made up his mind to run off with the circus which was coming the next Tuesday.

He turned his face away, sobbing, and his father, after standing by his bed a moment, went away without saying anything but, "Don't forget your prayers, Pony. You'll feel differently in the morning, I hope."

Pony fell asleep thinking how he would come back to the Boy's Town with the circus when he was grown up, and when he came out in the ring riding three horses bareback he would see his father and mother and sisters in one of the lower seats. They would not know him, but he would know them, and he would send for them to come to the dressing-room, and would be very good to them, all but his mother; he would be very cold and stiff with her, though he would know that she was prouder of him than all the rest put together, and she would go away almost crying.

He began being cold and stiff with her the very next morning, although she was better than ever to him, and gave him waffles for breakfast with unsalted butter, and tried to pet him up. That whole day she kept trying to do things for him, but he would scarcely speak to her; and at night she came to him and said, "What makes you act so strangely, Pony? Are you offended with your mother?"

"Yes, I am!" said Pony, haughtily, and he twitched away

from where she was sitting on the side of his bed, leaning over him.

"On account of last night, Pony?" she asked, softly.

"I reckon you know well enough," said Pony, and he tried to be disgusted with her for her being such a hypocrite, but he had to set his teeth hard, hard, or he would have broken down crying.

"If it's for that, you mustn't, Pony, dear. You don't know how you frightened me. When your snowball hit me, I felt sure it was a bat, and I'm so afraid of bats, you know. I didn't mean to hurt my poor boy's feelings so, and you mustn't mind it any more, Pony."

She stooped down and kissed him on the forehead, but he did not move or say anything; only, after that he felt more forgiving towards his mother. He made up his mind to be good to her along with the rest when he came back with the circus. But still he meant to run off with the circus. He did not see how he could do anything else, for he had told all the boys that day that he was going to do it; and when they just laughed, and said: "Oh yes. Think you can fool your grandmother! It'll be like running off with the Indians," Pony wagged his head, and said they would see whether it would or not, and offered to bet them what they dared.

The morning of the circus day all the fellows went out to the corporation line to meet the circus procession. There were ladies and knights, the first thing, riding on spotted horses; and then a band chariot, all made up of swans and dragons. There were about twenty baggage wagons; but before you got to them there was the greatest thing of all. It was a chariot drawn by twelve Shetland ponies, and it was shaped like a big shell, and around in the bottom of the shell there

W. D. Howells

were little circus actors, boys and girls, dressed in their circus clothes, and they all looked exactly like fairies. They scarce seemed to see the fellows, as they ran alongside of their chariot, but Hen Billard and Archy Hawkins, who were always cutting up, got close enough to throw some peanuts to the circus boys, and some of the little circus girls laughed, and the driver looked around and cracked his whip at the fellows, and they all had to get out of the way then.

Jim Leonard said that the circus boys and girls were all stolen, and nobody was allowed to come close to them for fear they would try to send word to their friends. Some of the fellows did not believe it, and wanted to know how he knew it; and he said he read it in a paper; after that nobody could deny it. But he said that if you went with the circus men of your own free will they would treat you first-rate; only they would give you burnt brandy to keep you little; nothing else but burnt brandy would do it, but that would do it, sure.

Pony was scared at first when he heard that most of the circus fellows were stolen, but he thought if he went of his own accord he would be all right. Still, he did not feel so much like running off with the circus as he did before the circus came. He asked Jim Leonard whether the circus men made all the children drink burnt brandy; and Archy Hawkins and Hen Billard heard him ask, and began to mock him. They took him up between them, one by his arms and the other by the legs, and ran along with him, and kept saying, "Does it want to be a great big circus actor? Then it shall, so it shall," and, "We'll tell the circus men to be very careful of you, Pony dear!" till Pony wriggled himself loose and began to stone them.

After that they had to let him alone, for when a fellow began to stone you in the Boy's Town you had to let him alone, unless you were going to whip him, and the fellows only wanted to have a little fun with Pony. But what they did made him all the more resolved to run away with the circus, just to show them.

He helped to carry water for the circus men's horses, along with the boys who earned their admission that way. He had no need to do it, because his father was going to take him in, anyway; but Jim Leonard said it was the only way to get acquainted with the circus men. Still Pony was afraid to speak to them, and he would not have said a word to any of them if it had not been for one of them speaking to him first, when he saw him come lugging a great pail of water, and bending far over on the right to balance it.

"That's right," the circus man said to Pony. "If you ever fell into that bucket you'd drown, sure."

He was a big fellow, with funny eyes, and he had a white bulldog at his heels; and all the fellows said he was the one who guarded the outside of the tent when the circus began, and kept the boys from hooking in under the curtain.

Even then Pony would not have had the courage to say anything, but Jim Leonard was just behind him with another bucket of water, and he spoke up for him. "He wants to go with the circus."

They both set down their buckets, and Pony felt himself turning pale when the circus man came towards them. "Wants to go with the circus, heigh? Let's have a look at you." He took Pony by the shoulders and turned him slowly round, and looked at his nice clothes, and took him by the chin. "Orphan?" he asked.

Pony did not know what to say, but Jim Leonard nodded; perhaps he did not know what to say, either; but Pony felt as

W. D. Howells

if they had both told a lie.

"Parents living?" The circus man looked at Pony, and Pony had to say that they were.

He gasped out, "Yes," so that you could scarcely hear him, and the circus man said:

"Well, that's right. When we take an orphan, we want to have his parents living, so that we can go and ask them what sort of a boy he is."

He looked at Pony in such a friendly, smiling way that Pony took courage to ask him whether they would want him to drink burnt brandy.

"What for?"

"To keep me little."

"Oh, I see." The circus man took off his hat and rubbed his forehead with a silk handkerchief, which he threw into the top of his hat before he put it on again. "No, I don't know as we will. We're rather short of giants just now. How would you like to drink a glass of elephant milk every morning and grow into an eight-footer?"

Pony said he didn't know whether he would like to be quite so big; and then the circus man said perhaps he would rather go for an India-rubber man; that was what they called the contortionists in those days.

"Let's feel of you again." The circus man took hold of Pony and felt his joints. "You're put together pretty tight; but I reckon we could make you do if you'd let us take you apart with a screw-driver and limber up the pieces with rattlesnake oil. Wouldn't like it, heigh? Well, let me see!" The circus man thought a moment, and then he said: "How would double-somersaults on four horses bareback do?"

Pony said that would do, and then the circus man said: "Well, then, we've just hit it, because our double-somersault, four-horse bareback is just going to leave us, and we want a new one right away. Now, there's more than one way of joining a circus, but the best way is to wait on your front steps with your things all packed up, and the procession comes along at about one o'clock in the morning and picks you up. Which'd you rather do?"

Pony pushed his toe into the turf, as he always did when he was ashamed, but he made out to say he would rather wait out on the front steps.

"Well, then, that's all settled," said the circus man. "We'll be along," and he was going away with his dog, but Jim Leonard called after him:

"You hain't asked him whereabouts he lives."

The circus man kept on, and he said, without looking around, "Oh, that's all right. We've got somebody that looks after that."

"It's the magician," Jim Leonard whispered to Pony, and they walked away.

W. D. Howells

IX

HOW PONY DID NOT QUITE
GET OFF WITH THE CIRCUS

A crowd of the fellows had been waiting to know what the boys had been talking about to the circus man; but Jim Leonard said: "Don't you tell, Pony Baker!" and he started to run, and that made Pony run, too, and they both ran till they got away from the fellows.

"You have got to keep it a secret; for if a lot of fellows find it out the constable'll get to know it, and he'll be watching out around the corner of your house, and when the procession comes along and he sees you're really going he'll take you up, and keep you in jail till your father comes and bails you out. Now, you mind!"

Pony said, "Oh, I won't tell anybody," and when Jim Leonard said that if a circus man was to feel *him* over, that way, and act so kind of pleasant and friendly, he would be too proud to speak to anybody, Pony confessed that he knew it was a great thing all the time.

"The way'll be," said Jim Leonard, "to keep in with him, and he'll keep the others from picking on you; they'll be afraid to, on account of his dog. You'll see, he'll be the one to come for you to-night; and if the constable is there the dog won't let him touch you. I never thought of that."

Perhaps on account of thinking of it now Jim Leonard felt free to tell the other fellows how Pony was going to run off, for when a crowd of them came along he told them. They said it was splendid, and they said that if they could make their mothers let them, or if they could get out of the house without their mothers knowing it, they were going to sit up with Pony and watch out for the procession, and bid him good-bye.

At dinner-time he found out that his father was going to take him and all his sisters to the circus, and his father and mother were so nice to him, asking him about the procession and everything, that his heart ached at the thought of running away from home and leaving them. But now he had to do it; the circus man was coming for him, and he could not back out; he did not know what would happen if he did. It seemed to him as if his mother had done everything she could to make it harder for him. She had stewed chicken for dinner, with plenty of gravy, and hot biscuits to sop in, and peach preserves afterwards; and she kept helping him to more, because she said boys that followed the circus around got dreadfully hungry. The eating seemed to keep his heart down; it was trying to get into his throat all the time; and he knew that she was being good to him, but if he had not known it he would have believed his mother was just doing it to mock him.

Pony had to go to the circus with his father and sisters, and to get on his shoes and a clean collar. But a crowd of the fellows were there at the tent door to watch out whether the circus man would say anything to him when he went in; and Jim Leonard rubbed up against him, when the man passed with his dog and did not even look at Pony, and said: "He's

W. D. Howells

just pretending. He don't want your father to know. He'll be round for you, sure. I saw him kind of smile to one of the other circus men."

It was a splendid circus, and there were more things than Pony ever saw in a circus before. But instead of hating to have it over, it seemed to him that it would never come to an end. He kept thinking and thinking, and wondering whether he would like to be a circus actor; and when the one came out who rode four horses bareback and stood on his head on the last horse, and drove with the reins in his teeth, Pony thought that he never could learn to do it; and if he could not learn he did not know what the circus men would say to him. It seemed to him that it was very strange he had not told that circus man that he didn't know whether he could do it or not; but he had not, and now it was too late.

A boy came around calling lemonade, and Pony's father bought some for each of the children, but Pony could hardly taste his.

"What is the matter with you, Pony? Are you sick?" his father asked.

"No. I don't care for any; that's all. I'm well," said Pony; but he felt very miserable.

After supper Jim Leonard came round and went up to Pony's room with him to help him pack, and he was so gay about it and said he only wished *he* was going, that Pony cheered up a little. Jim had brought a large square of checked gingham that he said he did not believe his mother would ever want, and that he would tell her he had taken if she asked for it. He said it would be the very thing for Pony to carry his clothes in, for it was light and strong and would hold a lot. He helped Pony to choose his things out of his bureau drawers: a pair of stockings and a pair of white pantaloons and a blue roundabout, and a collar, and two handkerchiefs. That was all he said Pony would need, because he would have his circus clothes right away, and there was no use taking things that he would never wear.

Jim did these up in the square of gingham, and he tied it across cater-cornered twice, in double knots, and showed Pony how he could put his hand through and carry it just as easy. He hid it under the bed for him, and he told Pony that if he was in Pony's place he should go to bed right away or pretty soon, so that nobody would think anything, and maybe he could get some sleep before he got up and went down to wait on the front steps for the circus to come along. He promised to be there with the other boys and keep them from fooling or making a noise, or doing anything to wake his father up, or make the constable come. "You see, Pony," he said, "if you can run off this year, and come back with the circus next year, then a whole lot of fellows can run off. Don't you see that?"

Pony said he saw that, but he said he wished some of the other fellows were going now, because he did not know any of the circus boys and he was afraid he might feel kind of lonesome. But Jim Leonard said he would soon get acquainted, and, anyway, a year would go before he knew it, and then if the other fellows could get off he would have plenty of company.

As soon as Jim Leonard was gone Pony undressed and got into bed. He was not sleepy, but he thought maybe it would be just as well to rest a little while before the circus procession came along for him; and, anyway, he could not bear to go down-stairs and be with the family when he was going to leave them so soon, and not come back for a whole year.

After a good while, or about the time he usually came in from playing, he heard his mother saying: "Where in the world is Pony? Has he come in yet? Have you seen him, girls? Pony! Pony!" she called.

But somehow Pony could not get his voice up out of his throat; he wanted to answer her, but he could not speak. He heard her say, "Go out to the front steps, girls, and see if you can see him," and then he heard her coming up the stairs; and she came into his room, and when she saw him lying there in bed she said: "Why, I believe in my heart the child's asleep! Pony! Are you awake?"

Pony made out to say no, and his mother said: "My! what a fright you gave me! Why didn't you answer me? Are you sick, Pony? Your father said you didn't seem well at the circus; and you didn't eat any supper, hardly."

Pony said he was first-rate, but he spoke very low, and his mother came up and sat down on the side of his bed.

"What is the matter, child?" She bent over and felt his forehead. "No, you haven't got a bit of fever," she said, and she kissed him, and began to tumble his short black hair in the way she had, and she got one of his hands between her two, and kept rubbing it. "But you've had a long, tiresome day, and that's why you've gone to bed, I suppose. But if you feel the least sick, Pony, I'll send for the doctor."

Pony said he was not sick at all; just tired; and that was true; he felt as if he never wanted to get up again.

His mother put her arm under his neck, and pressed her face close down to his, and said very low: "Pony, dear, you don't feel hard towards your mother for what she did the other night?"

He knew she meant boxing his ears, when he was not to blame, and he said: "Oh no," and then he threw his arms round her neck and cried; and she told him not to cry, and that she would never do such a thing again; but she was really so frightened she did not know what she was doing.

When he quieted down she said: "Now say your prayers, Pony, 'Our Father,'" and she said "Our Father" all through with him, and after that, "Now I lay me," just as when he was a very little fellow. After they had finished she stooped over and kissed him again, and when he turned his face into his pillow she kept smoothing his hair with her hand for about a minute. Then she went away.

Pony could hear them stirring about for a good while downstairs. His father came in from up-town at last and asked:

"Has Pony come in?" and his mother said:

"Yes, he's up in bed. I wouldn't disturb him, Henry. He's asleep by this time."

His father said: "I don't know what to make of the boy. If he keeps on acting so strangely I shall have the doctor see him in the morning."

Pony felt dreadfully to think how far away from them he should be in the morning, and he would have given anything if he could have gone down to his father and mother and told them what he was going to do. But it did not seem as if he could.

By-and-by he began to be sleepy, and then he dozed off, but he thought it was hardly a minute before he heard the circus band, and knew that the procession was coming for him. He jumped out of bed and put on his things as fast as he could;

but his roundabout had only one sleeve to it, somehow, and he had to button the lower buttons of his trousers to keep it on. He got his bundle and stole down to the front door without seeming to touch his feet to anything, and when he got out on the front steps he saw the circus magician coming along. By that time the music had stopped and Pony could not see any procession. The magician had on a tall, peaked hat, like a witch. He took up the whole street, he was so wide in the black glazed gown that hung from his arms when he stretched them out, for he seemed to be groping along that way, with his wand in one hand, like a blind man.

He kept saying in a kind of deep, shaking voice: "It's all glory; it's all glory," and the sound of those words froze Pony's blood. He tried to get back into the house again, so that the magician should not find him, but when he felt for the door-knob there was no door there anywhere; nothing but a smooth wall. Then he sat down on the steps and tried to shrink up so little that the magician would miss him; but he saw his wide goggles getting nearer and nearer; and then his father and the doctor were standing by him looking down at him, and the doctor said:

"He has been walking in his sleep; he must be bled," and he got out his lancet, when Pony heard his mother calling: "Pony, Pony! What's the matter? Have you got the nightmare?" and he woke up, and found it was just morning.

The sun was shining in at his window, and it made him so glad to think that by this time the circus was far away and he was not with it, that he hardly knew what to do.

He was not very well for two or three days afterwards, and his mother let him stay out of school to see whether he was really going to be sick or not. When he went back most of the fellows had forgotten that he had been going to run off with the circus. Some of them that happened to think of it plagued him a little and asked how he liked being a circus actor.

Hen Billard was the worst; he said he reckoned the circus magician got scared when he saw what a whaler Pony was, and told the circus men that they would have to get a new tent to hold him; and that was the reason why they didn't take him. Archy Hawkins said: "How long did you have to wait on the front steps, Pony, dear?" But after that he was pretty good to him, and said he reckoned they had better not any of them pretend that Pony had not tried to run off if they had not been up to see.

Pony himself could never be exactly sure whether he had waited on the front steps and seen the circus magician or not. Sometimes it seemed all of it like a dream, and sometimes only part of it. Jim Leonard tried to help him make it out, but they could not. He said it was a pity he had overslept himself, for if he had come to bid Pony good-bye, the way he said, then he could have told just how much of it was a dream and how much was not.

W. D. Howells

X

THE ADVENTURES THAT PONY'S COUSIN, FRANK BAKER, HAD WITH A POCKETFUL OF MONEY

Very likely Pony Baker would not have tried to run off any more if it had not been for Jim Leonard. He was so glad he had not got off with the circus that he did not mind any of the things at home that used to vex him; and it really seemed as if his father and mother were trying to act better. They were a good deal taken up with each other, and sometimes he thought they let him do things they would not have let him do if they had noticed what he asked. His mother was fonder of him than ever, and if she had not kissed him so much before the fellows he would not have cared, for when they were alone he liked to have her pet him. But one thing was, he could never get her to like Jim Leonard, or to believe that Jim was not leading him into mischief whenever they were off together. She was always wanting him to go with his cousin Frank, and he would have liked to ask Frank about running off, and whether a fellow had better do it; but he was ashamed, and especially after he heard his father tell how splendidly Frank had behaved with two thousand dollars he was bringing from the city to the Boy's Town; Pony was afraid that Frank would despise him, and he did not hardly feel fit to go with Frank, anyway.

Frank Baker was one of those fellows that every mother would feel her boy was safe with. She would be sure that no crowd he was in was going to do any harm or come to any, for he would have an anxious eye out for everybody, and he would stand between the crowd and the mischief that a crowd of boys nearly always wants to do. His own mother felt easy about the younger children when they were with Frank; and in a place where there were more chances for a boy to get sucked under mill-wheels, and break through ice, and fall from bridges, or have his fingers taken off by machinery than any other place I ever heard of, she no more expected anything to happen to them, if he had them in charge, than if she had them in charge herself.

As there were a good many other children in the family, and Mrs. Baker did her own work, like nearly every mother in the Boy's Town, Frank almost always had some of them in charge. When he went hunting, or fishing, or walnutting, or berrying, or in swimming, he usually had one or two younger brothers with him; if he had only one, he thought he was having the greatest kind of a time.

He did not mind carrying his brother on his back when he got tired, although it was not exactly the way to steal on game, and the gun was a heavy enough load, anyway; but if he had not got many walnuts, or any at all—as sometimes happened—it was not a great hardship to haul his brother home in the wagon. To be sure, when he wanted to swim out with the other big boys it was pretty trying to have to keep an eye on his brother, and see that he did not fall into the water from the bank where he left him.

He was a good deal more anxious about other boys than he was about himself, and once he came near getting drowned through his carelessness. It was in winter, and the canal basin had been frozen over; then most of the water was let out

W. D. Howells

from under the ice, and afterwards partly let in again. This lifted the ice-sheet, but not back to its old level, and the ice that clung to the shores shelved steeply down to the new level. Frank stepped on this shore ice to get a shinny-ball, and slipped down to the edge of the ice-sheet, which he would be sure to go under into the water. He holloed with all his might, and by good luck some people came and reached him a stick, by which he pulled himself out.

The scare of it haunted him for long after, but not so much for himself. Whenever he was away from home in the winter he would see one of his younger brothers slipping down the shore ice and going under the ice-sheet, and he would break into a cold sweat at the idea. This shows just the worrying kind of boy Frank was; and it shows how used he was to having care put upon him, and how he would even borrow trouble when he had none.

It generally happens with any one who makes himself useful that other people make him useful, too, and all the neighbors put as much trust in Frank as his mother, and got him to do a good many things that they would not have got other boys to do. They could not look into his face, a little more careworn than it ought to be at his age, without putting perfect faith in him, and trying to get something out of him. That was how he came to do so many errands for mothers who had plenty of boys of their own; and he seemed to be called on in any sort of trouble or danger, when the fathers were up-town, and was always chasing pigs or cows out of other people's gardens, and breaking up their hens from setting, or going up trees with hives to catch their bees when they swarmed.

I suppose this was how he came to be trusted with that pocketful of money, and why he had a young brother along to double his care at the time.

The money was given him in the city, as the Boy's Town boys always called the large place about twenty miles away, where Frank went once with his mother when he was eleven years old. She was going to take passage there on a steamboat and go up the Ohio River to visit his grandmother with his sisters, while Frank was to go back the same day to the Boy's Town with one of his young brothers.

They all drove down to the city together in the carriage which one of his uncles had got from the livery stable, with a driver who was to take Frank and his brother home. This uncle had been visiting Frank's father and mother, and it was his boat that she was going on. It lay among a hundred other boats, which had their prows tight together along the landing for half a mile up and down the sloping shore. It was one of the largest boats of all, and it ran every week from Cincinnati to Pittsburgh, and did not take any longer for the round trip than an ocean steamer takes now for the voyage from New York to Liverpool.

The children all had dinner on board, such a dinner as there never was in any house: roast beef and roast chicken; beefsteak and ham in chafing-dishes with lamps burning under them to keep them hot; pound-cake with frosting on, and pies and pickles, corn-bread and hot biscuit; jelly that kept shaking in moulds; ice-cream and Spanish pudding; coffee and tea, and I do not know what all.

When the children had eaten all they could hold, and made their uncle laugh till he almost cried, to see them trying to eat everything, their mother went ashore with them, and walked up the landing towards the hotel where the carriage was left, so as to be with Frank and his little brother as long as she could before they started home. She was about one of the best mothers in the Boy's Town, and Frank hated to have her go away even on a visit.

She kept giving him charges about all the things at home, and how he must take good care of his little brothers, and see that the garden gate was fastened so that the cows could not get in, and feed the chickens regularly, and put the cat out every night, and not let the dog sleep under his bed; and they were so busy talking and feeling sorry that they got to the hotel before they knew it.

There, whom should they see but one of the Boy's Town merchants, who was in the city on business, and who seemed as glad to meet them as if they were his own relations. They were glad, too, for it made them feel as if they had got back to the Boy's Town when he came up and spoke to Mrs. Baker. They had started from home after a very early breakfast, and she said it seemed as if they had been gone a year already. The merchant told her that he had been looking everywhere for somebody he knew who was going to the Boy's Town; and then he told Mrs. Baker that he had two thousand dollars which he wanted to send home to his partner, and he asked her if she could take it for him when she went back.

"Well, indeed, indeed, I'm thankful I'm not going, Mr. Bushell!" Mrs. Baker said. "And I wouldn't have supposed I could be, I'm so homesick. I'm going up the river on a visit to mother; but if I was going straight back, I wouldn't take your two thousand dollars for the half of it. I would be afraid of losing it, or getting robbed and murdered. I don't know what wouldn't happen. I would be happy to oblige you, but indeed, indeed I couldn't!"

The merchant said he was sorry, but if she was not going home he supposed he would have to find some one who was. It was before the days of sending money by express, or telegraphing it, and the merchant told her he was afraid to trust the money in the mail. He asked her who was going to take her carriage home, and she told him the name of the driver from the livery stable in the Boy's Town, who had come to the city with them.

Mr. Bushell seemed dreadfully disappointed, but when she went on to say how anxious she was that the driver should get Frank and his brother home before dark, he brightened up all of a sudden, and he asked, "Is Frank going back?" and he looked down into Frank's face and smiled, as most people did when they looked into Frank's face, and he asked, "What's the reason Frank couldn't take it?"

Mrs. Baker put her arm across Frank's breast and pulled him away, and said, "Indeed, indeed, the child just sha'n't, and that's all about it!"

But Mr. Bushell took the boy by the arm and laughed. "Let's feel how deep your pants' pocket is," he said; and he put his hand into the pocket of Frank's nankeen trousers and felt; and then, before Mrs. Baker could stop him, he drew a roll of bank-notes out of his own pocket and pushed it into Frank's. "There, it's just a fit! Do you think you'd lose it?"

"No, he wouldn't lose it," said his mother, "and that's just it! He'd worry about it every minute, and I would worry about him!"

She tried to make the merchant take the money back, but he kept joking; and then he turned serious, and told her that the money had to be put in the bank to pay a note, and he did not know any way to get it to his partner if she would not let Frank take it; that he was at his wits' end. He said he would as lief trust it with Frank as with any man he knew; that nobody would think the boy had any money with him; and he fairly begged her to let Frank take it for him.

W. D. Howells

He talked to her so much that she began to give way a little. She felt proud of his being willing to trust Frank, and at last she consented. Mr. Bushell explained that he wished his partner to have the money that evening, and she had to agree to let Frank carry it to him as soon as he got home.

The Boy's Town was built on two sides of a river. Mr. Bushell's store was across the river from where the Bakers lived, and she said she did not want the child to have to go through the bridge after dark. Perhaps it was her anxiety about this that began the whole trouble; for when the driver came with the carriage, she could not help asking him if he was sure to get home before sundown. That made him drive faster than he might have done, perhaps; at any rate, he set off at a quick trot after Mr. Bushell had helped put the two boys in. Mrs. Baker gathered her little girls together and went back to the boat with her heart in her mouth, as she afterwards said.

The driver got out of the city without trouble, but when he came to the smooth turnpike road, it seemed to Frank that the horses kept going faster and faster, till they were fairly flying over the ground. The driver pulled and pulled at the reins, and people began to hollo, "Look out where you're going!" when they met them or passed them, and all at once Frank began to think the horses were running away. He had not much chance to think about it, though, he was so busy keeping his little brother from bouncing off the seat and out of the carriage, and in feeling if Mr. Bushell's money was safe; and he was not certain that they were running away till he saw people stopping and staring, and then starting after the carriage.

The horses tore along for two or three miles; they thundered through the covered bridge on Mill's Creek, and passed the Four-Mile House. By the time they reached the little village beyond it they had the turnpike to themselves; every team coming and going drove into the gutter.

At the village a large, fat butcher, who was sitting tilted back in a chair at the door of his shop, saw the carriage coming in a whirlwind of dust, and he knew what the matter was. There was a horse standing at the hitching rail, and the butcher just had time to untie him and jump into the saddle when the runaways flew by. He took after them as fast as his horse could go, and overhauled them at the end of the next bridge and brought them to a stand.

It had really been nothing but a race against time. No one was hurt; the horses were pretty badly blown, that was all; but the carriage was so much shaken up that it had to be left at a wagon-shop, where it could not be mended till morning. The two boys were taken back to Four-Mile House, where they would have to pass the night.

Frank worried about his father, who would be expecting them home that evening; but he was glad his mother did not know what had happened. He was thankful enough when he felt his brother all over and found him safe and sound, and then put his hand on his pocket and found that Mr. Bushell's money was still there. He did not eat very much supper, and he went to bed early, after he had put his brother in bed and seen him fall asleep almost before he got through his prayers.

Frank was very tired, and pretty sore from the jouncing in the carriage; but he was too worried to be sleepy. He began to think, What if some one should get Mr. Bushell's money away from him in the night, while he was asleep? And then he was glad that he did not feel like sleeping. He got up and put on his clothes and sat down by the window, listening to his brother's breathing and looking out into the dark at the heat-lightning in the west. The day had been very hot and the night was close, without a breath of wind. By-and-by all the noises about the house died away, and he knew everybody had gone to bed. The lantern under the tavern porch threw a dim light out into the road; some dogs barked away off. There was no other sound, and the stillness was awful. He kept his hand on the pocket that had the money in it.

After a while Frank began to feel very drowsy, and he thought he would lie down again, but he promised himself he would not sleep, and he did not undress; for if he took his pantaloons off, he did not know how he could make sure every minute that the money was safe, unless he put it under his pillow. He was afraid if he did that he might forget it in the morning, and leave it when he got up.

He stretched himself on the bed beside his brother, and it seemed to him that it was hardly a second before he heard a loud crash that shook the whole house; and the room looked full of fire. Another crash came, and then another, with a loud, stony kind of rolling noise that seemed to go round the world. Then he knew that he had been asleep, and that this dreadful noise was the swift coming of a thunder-storm.

It was the worst storm that was ever known in Mill Creek Valley, so the people said afterwards, but as yet it was only beginning. The thunder was deafening, and it never stopped a moment. The lightning hardly stopped, either; it filled the room with a quivering blaze; at times, when it died down, the night turned black as ink, and then a flash came that lit up the fields outside, and showed every stick and stone as bright as the brightest day.

Frank was dazed at first by the glare and the noise; then he jumped out of bed, and tried for two things: whether the money was still safe in his pocket, and whether his brother was alive. He never could tell which he found out first; as soon as he knew, he felt a little bit better, but still his cheerfulness was not anything to brag of.

If his brother was alive, it seemed to be more than any one else in the house was besides himself. He could not hear a soul stirring, although in that uproar there might have been a full-dress parade of the Butler Guards in the tavern, firing off their guns, and he could not have heard them. He looked out in the entry, but it was all dark there except when he let the flashes of his room into it. He thought he would light his candle, for company, and so that the lightning would not be so awfully bright. He found his candlestick easily enough— he could have found a pin in that glare—but there were no matches.

So he decided to get along without the candle. Every now and then he put his hand in his pocket, or on the bulge outside, to make sure of the money; and whenever a very bright flash came, he would listen for his brother's breathing, to tell whether he had been struck by lightning or not. But it kept thundering so that sometimes he could not hear. Then Frank would shake him till the boy gave a sort of snort, and that proved that he was still alive; or he would put his ear to his brother's breast, and listen whether his heart was beating.

It always was, and by-and-by the rain began to fall. It fell in perfect sheets, and the noise it made could be heard through the thunder. But Frank had always heard that after it began to rain, a thunder-storm was not so dangerous, and the air got fresher. Still, it blazed and bellowed away, he could never tell how long, and it seemed to him that he must have felt a thousand times for Mr. Bushell's money, and tried a thousand times to find whether his brother had been struck by lightning or not. Once or twice he thought he would call for help; but he did not think he could make anybody hear, and he was too much ashamed to do it, anyway.

W. D. Howells

Between the times of feeling for the money and seeing whether his brother was alive, he thought about his mother: how frightened she would be if she knew what had happened to him and his brother, after they left her. And he thought of his father: how troubled he must be at their not getting home. It seemed to him that he must be to blame, somehow, but he could not understand how, exactly; and he could not think of any way to help it.

He wondered if the storm was as bad on the river and in the Boy's Town, and whether the lightning would strike the boat or the house; the house had a lightning-rod, but the boat could not have one, of course. He felt pretty safe about his father and the older-younger brother who had been left at home with him; but he was not sure about his mother and sisters, and he tried to imagine what people did on a steamboat in a thunder-storm.

After a long time had passed, and he thought it must be getting near morning, he lay down again beside his brother, and fell into such a heavy sleep that he did not wake till it was broad day, and the sun was making as much blaze in the curtainless tavern-room as the lightning had made. The storm was over, and everything was as peaceful as if there had never been any such thing as a storm in the world. The first thing he did was to make a grab for his pocket. The money was still there, and his brother sleeping as soundly as ever.

After breakfast, the livery-stable man came with the carriage, which he had got mended, and Frank started home with his brother once more. But they had sixteen miles to go before they would reach the Boy's Town, and the carriage had been so badly shattered, or else the driver was so much afraid of the horses, that he would not let them go at more than a walk. Frank was anxious to get home on his father's account; still he would rather get home safe, and he did not try to hurry the driver, for fear they might not get home at all.

It was four o'clock in the afternoon when they stopped at his father's house. His older-younger brother, and the hired girl, whom his mother had got to keep house while she was gone on her visit, came out and took his little brother in; and the girl told Frank his father had just been there to see whether he had got back. Then he knew that his father must have been as anxious as he had been afraid he was. He did not wait to go inside; he only kicked off the shoes he wore to the city and started off for his father's office as fast as his bare feet could carry him.

He found his father at the door. He did not say very much, but Frank could see by his face that he had been worrying; and afterwards he said that he was just going round to the livery stable the next minute to get another team, and go down towards the city to see what had become of them all. Frank told him what had happened, and his father put his arms round him, but still did not say much. He did not say anything at all about Mr. Bushell's money or seem to think about it till Frank asked:

"I'd better take it right straight over to his store, hadn't I, father?"

His father said he reckoned he had, and Frank started away on the run again. He wanted to get rid of that money so badly, for it was all he had to worry about, after he had got rid of his brother, that he was out of breath, almost, by the time he reached Mr. Bushell's store. But even then he could not get rid of the money. Mr. Bushell had told him to give it to his partner, but his partner had gone out into the country, and was not to be back till after supper.

Frank did not know what to do. He did not dare to give it to

W. D. Howells

any one else in the store, and it seemed to him that the danger of having it got worse every minute. He hung about a good while, and kept going in and out of the store, but at last he thought the best thing would be to go home and ask his father; and that was what he did.

By this time his father had gone home to supper, and he found him there with his two younger brothers, feeling rather lonesome, with Frank's mother and his sisters all away. But they cheered up together, and his father said he had done right not to leave the money, and he would just step over, after supper, and give it himself to Mr. Bushell's partner. He took the roll of bills from Frank and put it into his own pocket, and went on eating his supper, but when they were done he gave the bills back to the boy.

"After all, Frank, I believe I'll let you take that money to Mr. Bushell's partner. He trusted it to you, and you ought to have the glory; you've had the care. Do you think you'll be afraid to come home through the bridge after sunset?"

The bridge was one of those old-fashioned, wooden ones, roofed in and sided up, and it stretched from shore to shore, like a tunnel, on its piers. It was rather dim, even in the middle of the brightest day, and none of the boys liked to be caught in it after sunset.

Frank said he did not believe he should be afraid, for it seemed to him that if he had got through a runaway, and such a thunder-storm as that was the night before, without harm, he could surely get through the bridge safely. There was not likely to be anybody in it, at the worst, but Indian Jim, or Solomon Whistler, the crazy man, and he believed he could run by them if they offered to do anything to him. He meant to walk as slowly as he could, until he reached the bridge, and then just streak through it.

That was what he did, and it was still quite light when he reached Mr. Bushell's store. His partner was there, sure enough, this time, and Frank gave him the money, and told him how he had been so long bringing it. The merchant thanked him, and said he was rather young to be trusted with so much money, but he reckoned Mr. Bushell knew what he was about.

"Did he count it when he gave it to you?" he asked.

"No, he didn't," said Frank.

"Did you?"

"I didn't have a chance. He put it right into my pocket, and I was afraid to take it out."

Mr. Bushell's partner laughed, and Frank was going away, so as to get through the bridge before it was any darker, but Mr. Bushell's partner said, "Just hold on a minute, won't you, Frank, till I count this," and he felt as if his heart had jumped into his throat.

What if he had lost some of the money? What if somebody had got it out of his pocket, while he was so dead asleep, and taken part of it? What if Mr. Bushell had made a mistake, and not given him as much as he thought he had? He hardly breathed while Mr. Bushell's partner slowly counted the bank-notes. It took him a long time, and he had to wet his finger a good many times, and push the notes to keep them from sticking together. At last he finished, and he looked at Frank over the top of his spectacles. "Two thousand?" he asked.

"That's what Mr. Bushell said," answered the boy, and he could hardly get the words out.

"Well, it's all here," said Mr. Bushell's partner, and he put the money in his pocket, and Frank turned and went out of the store.

He felt light, light as cotton, and gladder than he almost ever was in his life before. He was so glad that he forgot to be afraid in the bridge. The fellows who were the most afraid always ran through the bridge, and those who tried not to be afraid walked fast and whistled. Frank did not even think to whistle.

His father was sitting out on the front porch when he reached home, and he asked Frank if he had got rid of his money, and what Mr. Bushell's partner had said. Frank told him all about it, and after a while his father asked, "Well, Frank, do you like to have the care of money?"

"I don't believe I do, father."

"Which was the greater anxiety to you last night, Mr. Bushell's money, or your brother?"

Frank had to think awhile. "Well, I suppose it was the money, father. You see, it wasn't my own money."

"And if it had been your own money, you wouldn't have been anxious about it? You wouldn't have cared if you had lost it, or somebody had stolen it from you?"

Frank thought again, and then he said he did not believe he had thought about that.

"Well, think about it now."

Frank tried to think, and at last he said. "I reckon I should have cared."

"And if it had been your own money, would you have been more anxious about it than about your brother?"

This time Frank was more puzzled than ever; he really did not know what to say.

His father said: "The trouble with money is, that people who have a great deal of it seem to be more anxious about it than they are about their brothers, and they think that the things it can buy are more precious than the things which all the money in the world cannot buy." His father stood up. "Better go to bed, Frank. You must be tired. There won't be any thunder-storm to-night, and you haven't got a pocketful of money to keep you awake."

XI

HOW JIM LEONARD PLANNED
FOR PONY BAKER TO RUN OFF ON A RAFT

Now we have got to go back to Pony Baker again. The summer went along till it got to be September, and the fellows were beginning to talk about when school would take up. It was almost too cold to go in swimming; that is, the air made you shiver when you came out, and before you got your clothes on; but if you stood in the water up to your chin, it seemed warmer than it did on the hottest days of summer. Only now you did not want to go in more than once a day, instead of four or five times. The fellows were gathering chinquapin acorns most of the time, and some of them were getting ready to make wagons to gather walnuts in. Once they went out to the woods for pawpaws, and found about a bushel; they put them in cornmeal to grow, but they were so green that they only got rotten. The boys found an old shanty in the woods where the farmer made sugar in the spring, and some of the big fellows said they were coming out to sleep in it, the first night they got.

It was this that put Jim Leonard in mind of Pony's running off again. All the way home he kept talking to Pony about it, and Pony said he was going to do it yet, some time, but when Jim Leonard wanted him to tell the time, he would only say,

"You'll see," and wag his head.

Then Jim Leonard mocked him and dared him to tell, and asked him if he would take a dare. After that he made up with him, and said if Pony would run off he would run off, too; and that the way for them to do would be to take the boards of that shanty in the woods and build a raft. They could do it easily, because the boards were just leaned up against the ridge-pole, and they could tie them together with pawpaw switches, they were so tough, and then some night carry the raft to the river, after the water got high in the fall, and float down on it to the city.

"Why, does the river go past the city?" Pony asked.

"Of course it does," said Jim Leonard, and he laughed at Pony. "It runs into the Ohio there. Where's your geography?"

Pony was ashamed to say that he did not suppose that geography had anything to do with the river at the Boy's Town, for it was not down on the map, like Behring Straits and the Isthmus of Suez. But he saw that Jim Leonard really knew something. He did not see the sense of carrying the raft two miles through the woods when you could get plenty of drift-wood on the river shore to make a raft of. But he did not like to say it for fear Jim Leonard would think he was afraid to be in the woods after dark, and after that he came under him more than ever. Most of the fellows just made fun of Jim Leonard, because they said he was a brag, but Pony began to believe everything he said when he found out that he knew where the river went to; Pony had never even thought.

Jim was always talking about their plan of running off together, now; and he said they must fix everything so that it would not fail this time. If they could only get to the city once, they could go for cabin-boys on a steamboat that was bound for New Orleans; and down the Mississippi they could easily hide on some ship that was starting for the Spanish Main, and then they would be all right. Jim knew about the Spanish Main from a book of pirate stories that he had. He had a great many books and he was always reading them. One was about Indians, and one was about pirates, and one was about dreams and signs, and one was full of curious stories, and one told about magic and how to do jugglers' tricks; the other was a fortune-telling book. Jim Leonard had a paper from the city, with long stories in, and he had read a novel once; he could not tell the boys exactly what a novel was, but that was what it said on the back.

After Pony and he became such friends he told him everything that was in his books, and once, when Pony went to his house, he showed him the books. Pony was a little afraid of Jim Leonard's mother; she was a widow woman, and took in washing; she lived in a little wood-colored house down by the river-bank, and she smoked a pipe. She was a very good mother to Jim, and let him do whatever he pleased—go in swimming as much as he wanted to, stay out of school, or anything. He had to catch drift-wood for her to burn when the river was high; once she came down to the river herself and caught drift-wood with a long pole that had a nail in the end of it to catch on with.

By the time school took up Pony and Jim Leonard were such great friends that they asked the teacher if they might sit together, and they both had the same desk. When Pony's mother heard that, it seemed as if she were going to do something about it. She said to his father:

"I don't like Pony's going with Jim Leonard so much. He's had nobody else with him for two weeks, and now he's sitting with him in school."

Pony's father said, "I don't believe Jim Leonard will hurt Pony. What makes you like him, Pony?"

Pony said, "Oh, nothing," and his father laughed.

"It seems to be a case of pure affection. What do you talk about together?"

"Oh, dreams, and magic, and pirates," said Pony.

His father laughed, but his mother said, "I know hell put mischief in the child's head," and then Pony thought how Jim Leonard always wanted him to run off, and he felt ashamed; but he did not think that running off was mischief, or else all the boys would not be wanting to do it, and so he did not say anything.

His father said, "I don't believe there's any harm in the fellow. He's a queer chap."

"He's so low down," said Pony's mother.

"Well, he has a chance to rise, then," said Pony's father. "We may all be hurrahing for him for President some day." Pony could not always tell when his father was joking, but it seemed to him he must be joking now. "I don't believe Pony will get any harm from sitting with him in school, at any rate."

After that Pony's mother did not say anything, but he knew that she had taken a spite to Jim Leonard, and when he brought him home with him after school he did not bring him into the woodshed as he did with the other boys, but took him out to the barn. That got them to playing in the barn most of the time, and they used to stay in the hay-loft, where Jim Leonard told Pony the stories out of his books. It was good and warm there, and now the days were getting chilly towards evenings.

Once, when they were lying in the hay together, Jim Leonard said, all of a sudden, "I've thought of the very thing, Pony Baker."

Pony asked, "What thing?"

"How to get ready for running off," said Jim Leonard, and at that Pony's heart went down, but he did not like to show it, and Jim Leonard went on: "We've got to provision the raft, you know, for maybe we'll catch on an island and be a week getting to the city. We've got to float with the current, anyway. Well, now, we can make a hole in the hay here and hide the provisions till we're ready to go. I say we'd better begin hiding them right away. Let's see if we can make a place. Get away, Trip."

He was speaking to Pony's dog, that always came out into the barn with him and stayed below in the carriage-room, whining and yelping till they helped him up the ladder into the loft. Then he always lay in one corner, with his tongue out, and looking at them as if he knew what they were saying. He got up when Jim Leonard bade him, and Jim pulled away the hay until he got down to the loft floor.

"Yes, it's the very place. It's all solid, and we can put the things down here and cover them up with hay and nobody will notice. Now, to-morrow you bring out a piece of bread-and-butter with meat between, and I will, too, and then we will see how it will do."

Pony brought his bread-and-butter the next day. Jim said he intended to bring some hard-boiled eggs, but his mother kept looking, and he had no chance.

"Let's see whether the butter's sweet, because if it ain't the provisions will spoil before we can get off."

He took a bite, and he said, "My, that's nice!" and the first thing he knew he ate the whole piece up. "Well, never mind," he said, "we can begin to-morrow just as well."

The next day Jim Leonard brought a ham-bone, to cook greens with on the raft. He said it would be first-rate; and Pony brought bread-and-butter, with meat between. Then they hid them in the hay, and drove Trip away from the place. The day after that, when they were busy talking, Trip dug the provisions up, and, before they noticed, he ate up Pony's bread-and-butter and was gnawing Jim Leonard's ham-bone. They cuffed his ears, but they could not make him give it up, and Jim Leonard said:

"Well, let him have it. It's all spoilt now, anyway. But I'll tell you what, Pony—we've got to do something with that dog. He's found out where we keep our provisions, and now he'll always eat them. I don't know but what we'll have to kill him."

"Oh no!" said Pony. "I couldn't kill Trip!"

"Well, I didn't mean kill him, exactly; but do something. I'll tell you what—train him not to follow you to the barn when he sees you going."

Pony thought that would be a good plan, and he began the next day at noon. Trip tried to follow him to the barn, and Pony kicked at him, and motioned to stone him, and said: "Go home, sir! Home with you! Home, I say!" till his mother came to the back door.

"Why, what in the world makes you so cross with poor Trip,

W. D. Howells

Pony?" she asked.

"I'll teach him not to tag me round everywhere," said Pony.

His mother said: "Why, I thought you liked to have him with you?"

"I'm tired of it," said Pony; but when he put his mother off that way he felt badly, as if he had told her a lie, and he let Trip come with him and began to train him again the next day.

It was pretty hard work, and Trip looked at him so mournfully when he drove him back that he could hardly bear to do it; but Jim Leonard said it was the only way, and he must keep it up. At last Trip got so that he would not follow Pony to the barn. He would look at him when Pony started and wag his tail wistfully, and half jump a little, and then when he saw Pony frown he would let his tail drop and stay still, or walk off to the woodshed and keep looking around at Pony to see if he were in earnest. It made Pony's heart ache, for he was truly fond of Trip; but Jim Leonard said it was the only way, and so Pony had to do it.

They provisioned themselves a good many times, but after they talked a while they always got hungry, or Jim Leonard did, and then they dug up their provisions and ate them. Once when he came to spend Saturday afternoon with Pony he had great news to tell him. One of the boys had really run off. He was a boy that Pony had never seen, though he had heard of him. He lived at the other end of the town, below the bridge, and almost at the Sycamore Grove. He had the name of being a wild fellow; his father was a preacher, but he could not do anything with him.

Now, Jim Leonard said, Pony must run off right away, and

not wait for the river to rise, or anything. As soon as the river rose, Jim would follow him on the raft; but Pony must start first, and he must take the pike for the city, and sleep in fence corners. They must provision him, and not eat any of the things before he started. He must not take a bundle or anything, because if he did people would know he was running off, or maybe they would think he was a runaway slave from Kentucky, he was so dark-complexioned. At first Pony did not like it, because it seemed to him that Jim Leonard was backing out; but Jim Leonard said that if two of them started off at the same time, people would just know they were running off, and the constable would take them up before they could get across the corporation line. He said that very likely it would rain in less than a week, and then he could start after Pony on the raft, and be at the Ohio River almost as soon as Pony was.

He said, "Why, you ain't afraid, are you, Pony?" And Pony said he was not afraid; for if there was anything that a Boy's Town boy hated, it was to be afraid, and Pony hated it the worst of any, because he was sometimes afraid that he was afraid.

They fixed it that Pony was to sleep the next Friday night in the barn, and the next morning, before it was light, he was to fill his pockets with the provisions and run off.

Every afternoon he took out a piece of bread-and-butter with meat between and hid it in the hay, and Jim Leonard brought some eggs. He said he had no chance to boil them without his mother seeing, but he asked Pony if he did not know that raw eggs were first-rate, and when Pony said no, he said, "Well, they are." They broke one of the eggs when they were hiding them, and it ran over the bread-and-butter, but they wiped it off with hay as well as they could, and Jim Leonard said maybe it would help to keep it, anyway.

W. D. Howells

When he came round to Pony's house the next Friday afternoon from school he asked him if he had heard the news, and when Pony said no, he said that the fellow that ran off had been taken up in the city by the watchman. He was crying on the street, and he said he had nowhere to sleep, and had not had anything to eat since the night before.

Pony's heart seemed to be standing still. He had always supposed that as soon as he ran off he should be free from all the things that hindered and vexed him; and, although he expected to be sorry for his father and mother, he expected to get along perfectly well without them. He had never thought about where he should sleep at night after he got to the city, or how he should get something to eat.

"Now, you see, Pony," said Jim Leonard, "what a good thing it was that I thought about provisioning you before you started. What makes you look so?"

Pony said, "I'm not looking!"

Jim Leonard said, "You're not afraid, are you, just because that fellow got took up? You're not such a cowardy-calf as to want to back out now?"

The tears came into Pony's eyes.

"Cowardy-calf yourself, Jim Leonard! You've backed out long ago!"

"You'll see whether I've backed out," said Jim Leonard. "I'm coming round to sleep in the barn with you to-night, and help you to get a good start in the morning. And maybe I'll start myself to-morrow. I will if I can get anybody to help me make the raft and bring it through the woods. Now let's go up into the loft and see if the provisions are all safe."

They dug the provisions up out of the hay and Jim Leonard broke one of the eggs against the wall. It had a small chicken in it, and he threw it away. Another egg smelt so that they could hardly stand it.

"I don't believe these eggs are very good," said Jim Leonard. "I got them out of a nest that the hen had left; mother said I might have them all." He broke them one after another, and every one had a chicken in it, or else it was bad. "Well, never mind," he said. "Let's see what the bread-and-butter's like." He bit into a piece, but he did not swallow any. "Tastes kind of musty; from the hay, I reckon; and the meat seems kind of old. But they always give the sailors spoilt provisions, and this bread-and-butter will do you first-rate, Pony. You'll be so hungry you can eat anything. Say, you ain't afraid now, are you, Pony?"

"No, not now," said Pony, but he did not fire up this time as he did before at the notion of his being afraid.

Jim Leonard said, "Because, maybe I can't get mother to let me come here again. If she takes a notion, she won't. But I'm going to watch out, and as soon as supper's over, and I've got the cow into the lot, and the morning's wood in, I'm going to try to hook off. If I don't get here to stay all night with you I'll be around bright and early in the morning, to wake you and start you. It won't be light now much before six, anyway."

XII

HOW JIM LEONARD BACKED OUT,
AND PONY HAD TO GIVE IT UP

It all seemed very strange to Pony. First, Jim Leonard was going to run off with him on a raft, and then he was going to have Pony go by land and follow him on the raft; then suddenly he fixed it so that Pony was going alone, and he was going to pass the last night with him in the barn; and here, all at once, he was only coming, maybe, to see him off in the morning. It made Pony feel very forlorn, but he did not like to say anything for fear Jim Leonard would call him cowardy-calf.

It was near sunset, on a cool day in the beginning of October, and the wind was stirring the dry blades in the corn-patch at the side of the barn. They made a shivering sound, and it made Pony lonesomer and lonesomer. He did not want to run off, but he did not see how he could help it. Trip stood at the wood-house door, looking at him, but he did not dare to come to Pony as long as he was near the barn. But when Pony started towards the house Trip came running and jumping to him, and Pony patted him and said, "Poor Trip, poor old Trip!" He did not know when he should see such another dog as that.

The kitchen door was open, and a beautiful smell of frying supper was coming out. Pretty soon his mother came to the open door, and stood watching him patting Trip. "Well, have you made up with poor old Trip, Pony? Why don't you come in, child? You look so cold, out there."

Pony did not say anything, but he came into the kitchen and sat in a corner beyond the stove and watched his mother getting the supper. In the dining-room his sisters were setting the table and his father was reading by the lamp there. Pony would have given almost anything if something had happened just to make him tell what he was going to do, so that he could have been kept from doing it. He saw that his mother was watching him all the time, and she said: "What makes you so quiet, child?"

Pony said, "Oh, nothing," and his mother asked, "Have you been falling out with Jim Leonard?"

Pony said no, and then she said, "I almost wish you had, then. I don't think he's a bad boy, but he's a crazy fool, and I wish you wouldn't go with him so much. I don't like him."

All of a sudden Pony felt that he did not like Jim Leonard very much himself. It seemed to him that Jim Leonard had not used him very well, but he could not have told how.

After supper the great thing was how to get out to the barn without any one's noticing. Pony went to the woodshed door two or three times to look out. There were plenty of stars in the sky, but it seemed very dark, and he knew that it would be as black as pitch in the barn, and he did not see how he could ever dare to go out to it, much less into it. Every time he came back from looking he brought an armload of wood into the kitchen so that his mother would not notice.

The last time she said, "Why, you dear, good boy, what a lot of wood you're bringing for your mother," for usually Pony had to be told two or three times before he would get a single armload of wood.

When his mother praised him he was ashamed to look at her, and so he looked round, and he saw the lantern hanging by the mantel-piece. When he saw that lantern he almost wished that he had not seen it, for now he knew that his last excuse was gone, and he would really have to run off. If it had not been for the lantern he could have told Jim Leonard that he was afraid to go out to the barn on account of ghosts, for anybody would be afraid of ghosts; Jim Leonard said he was afraid of them himself. But now Pony could easily get the lantern and take it out to the barn with him, and if it was not dark the ghosts would not dare to touch you.

He tried to think back to the beginning of the time when he first intended to run off, and find out if there was not some way of not doing it; but he could not, and if Jim Leonard was to come to the barn the next morning to help him start, and should not find him there, Pony did not know what he would do. Jim Leonard would tell all the fellows, and Pony would never hear the last of it. That was the way it seemed to him, but his mind felt all fuzzy, and he could not think very clearly about it.

When his mother finished up her work in the kitchen he took the lantern from the nail and slipped up the back stairs to his little room, and then, after he heard his sisters going to bed and his father and mother talking together quietly, he lit the lantern and stole out to the barn with it. Nobody noticed him, and he got safely inside the barn. He used to like to carry the lantern very much, because it made the shadows of his legs, when he walked, go like scissors-blades, and that was fun; but that night it did not cheer him up, and it seemed as if nothing could cheer him up again. When Trip first saw him come out into the woodshed with the lantern he jumped up and pawed Pony and licked the lantern, he was so glad, but when Pony went towards the barn Trip stopped following him and went back into the wood-house very sadly. Pony would have given almost anything to have Trip come with him, only, as Jim Leonard said, Trip would whine or bark, or something, and then Pony would be found out and kept from running off.

The more he wanted to be kept from running off the more he knew he must not try to be, and he let Trip go back when he would have so gladly helped him up into the hay-loft and slept with him there. He would not have been afraid with Trip, and now he found that he was dreadfully afraid. The lantern-light was a charm against ghosts, but not against rats, and the first thing Pony knew when he got into the barn a rat ran across his foot. Trip would have kept the rats off. They seemed to just swarm in the loft when Pony got up there, and after he hung the lantern on a nail and lay down in the hay they did not mind him at all. They played all around, and two of them got up on their hind legs once and fought, or else danced, Pony could not tell which. He could not sleep, and after a while he felt the tears coming and he began to cry, and he kept sobbing, and could not stop himself.

When Pony's mother was ready to go to bed she said to Pony's father: "Did Pony say good-night to you?" and when he said no, she said, "But he must have gone to bed," and she ran up the stairs to see. She came down again in about half a second and she said, "He doesn't seem to be there," and she raced all through the house hunting for him. In the kitchen she saw that the lantern was gone and then she said: "I might have known he was up to some mischief, he was so quiet. This is some more of Jim Leonard's work. Henry, I want you to go right out and look for Pony. It's half-past nine."

Then Pony's father knew that it would be no use to talk and he started out. But the whole street was quiet, and all the houses were dark as if the people had gone to bed. He went up town and to all the places where the big boys were apt to play at night, and he found Hen Billard and Archy Hawkins, but neither of them had seen Pony since school. They were both sitting on Hen Billard's front steps, because Archy Hawkins was going to stay all night with him, and they were telling stories. When Pony's father asked about Pony and seemed anxious they tried to comfort him, but they could not think where Pony could be. They said perhaps Jim Leonard would know.

Then Pony's father went home, and the minute he opened the front door Pony's mother called out: "Have you found him?"

His father said: "No. Hasn't he come in yet?" and he told her how he had been looking everywhere, and she burst out crying.

"I know he's fallen into the canal and got drowned, or something," and she wrung her hands together; and then he said that Hen Billard and Archy Hawkins thought Jim Leonard would know, and he had only stopped to see whether Pony had happened to come in, and he was going straight to Jim Leonard's mother's house; and Pony's mother said: "Oh, go, go, go!" and fairly pushed him out of the house.

By this time it was ten o'clock and going on eleven, and all the town was as still as death, except the dogs. Pony's father kept on until he got down to the river-bank, where Jim Leonard's mother lived, and he had to knock and knock before he could make anybody hear. At last Jim Leonard's mother poked her head out of the window and asked who was there, and Pony's father told her.

He said: "Is Jim at home, Mrs. Leonard?" and she said:

"Yes, and fast asleep three hours ago. What makes you ask?"

Then he had to tell her. "We can't find Pony, and some of the boys thought Jim might know where he is. I'm sorry to disturb you, Mrs. Leonard. Good-night," and he went back home.

When he got there he found Pony's mother about crazy. He said now they must search the house thoroughly; and they went down into the cellar first, because she said she knew Pony had fallen down the stairs and killed himself. But he was not there, and then they hunted through all the rooms and looked under the tables and beds and into the cupboards and closets, and he was not there. Then they went into the wood-house and looked there, and up into the wood-house loft among the old stoves and broken furniture, and he was not there. Trip was there, and he made them think so of Pony that Pony's mother took on worse than she had yet.

"Now I'm going out to look in the barn," said Pony's father. "You stay quietly in the house, Lucy."

Trip started to go with Pony's father, but when he saw that he was going to the barn he was afraid to follow him, Pony had trained him so; and Pony's father went alone. He shaded the candle that he was carrying with his hand, and when he got into the barn he put it down and stood and looked and tried to think how he should do. It was dangerous to go around among the hay with the candle, and the lantern was gone.

Almost from the first Pony's father thought that he heard a strange noise like some one sobbing, and then it seemed to him that there was a light up in the loft. He holloed out: "Who's there?" and then the noise stopped, but the light kept

W. D. Howells

on. Pony's father holloed out again: "Pony! Is that you, Pony?" and then Pony answered, "Yes," and he began sobbing again.

In less than half a second Pony's father was up in the loft, and then down again and out of the barn and into the yard with Pony.

His mother was standing at the back door, for she could not bear to stay in the house, and Pony's father holloed to her: "Here he is, Lucy, safe and sound!" and Pony's mother holloed back:

"Well, don't touch him, Henry! Don't scold the child! Don't say a word to him! Oh, I could just fall on my knees!"

Pony's father came along, bringing Pony and the lantern. Pony's hair and clothes were all stuck full of pieces of hay, and his face was smeared with hay-dust which he had rubbed into it when he was crying. He had got some of Jim Leonard's mother's hen's eggs on him, and he did not smell very well. But his mother did not care how he looked or how he smelled. She caught him up into her arms and just fairly hugged him into the house, and there she sat down with him in her arms, and kissed his dirty face, and his hair all full of hay-sticks and spider-webs, and cried till it seemed as if she was never going to stop.

She would not let his father say anything to him, but after a while she washed him, and when she got him clean she made him up a bed on the lounge and put him to sleep there where she could see him. She said she was not going to sleep herself that night, but just stay up and realize that they had got Pony safe again.

One thing she did ask him, and that was: "What in the world

made you want to sleep in the barn, Pony?" and Pony was ashamed to say he was getting ready to run off. He began:

"Jim Leonard—" and his mother broke out:

"I knew it was some of Jim Leonard's work!" and she talked against Jim Leonard until Pony fell asleep, and said Pony should never speak to him again.

She and Pony's father sat up all night talking, and about daybreak he recollected that he had left the candle burning in the barn, and he ran out with all his might to get it before it set the barn on fire. But it had burned out without catching anything, and he was coming back to the house when he met Jim Leonard sneaking towards the barn door. He pounced on him, and caught him by the collar, and he said as savagely as he could: "What are you doing here, Jim?"

Jim Leonard was too scared to speak, and Pony's father hauled him to the house door, and holloed in to Pony's mother: "I've got Jim Leonard here, Lucy"; and she holloed back:

"Oh, well, take him away, and don't let me see the dreadful boy!" and Pony's father said:

"I'll take him home to his mother, and see what she has to say to him."

All the way down to the river-bank he did not say a word to Jim Leonard, but when they got to Jim Leonard's mother's house, there she was with her pipe in her mouth coming out to get chips to kindle the fire with, and she said:

"I'd like to know what you've got my boy by the collar for, Mr. Baker?"

W. D. Howells

Pony's father said: "I don't know myself; I'll let him tell you. Pony was hid in the barn last night, and I just now caught Jim prowling around on the outside. I should like to hear what he wanted."

Jim Leonard did not say anything. His mother gave him one look, and then she went into the house and came out with a table-knife in her hand.

She said, "I reckon I can get him to tell you," and she went to a pear-tree that there was before her house and cut a long sucker from the foot of it. She came up to Jim and then she said: "Tell!"

She did not have to say it twice, and in about half a second he told how Pony had intended to run off and how he put him up to it, and everything. Pony's father did not wait to see what Jim Leonard's mother did to Jim.

When Pony woke in the morning he heard his mother saying: "I could almost think he had bewitched the child."

His father said: "It really seems like a case of mesmeric influence."

Pony was sick for about a week after that. When he got better his father had a very solemn talk with him, and asked why he ever dreamed of running away from his home, where they all loved him so. Pony could not tell. All the things that he used to be so mad about were like nothing to him now, and he was ashamed of them. His father did not try hard to make him tell. He explained to him what a miserable boy he would have been if he had really got away, and said he hoped his night's experience in the barn would be a lesson to him.

That was what it turned out to be. But it seemed to be a lesson to his father and mother, too. They let him do more things, and his mother did not baby him so much before the boys. He thought she was trying to be a better mother to him, and, perhaps, she did not baby him so much because now he had a little brother for her to baby instead, that was born about a week after Pony tried to run off.

THE END

W. D. Howells

ABOUT THE AUTHOR

 **William Dean Howells** (March 1, 1837 – May 11, 1920) was an American realist author and literary critic.

Born in Martins Ferry, Ohio, originally Martinsville, to William Cooper and Mary Dean Howells, Howells was the second of eight children. His father was a newspaper editor and printer, and the father moved frequently around Ohio. Howells began to help his father with typesetting and printing work at an early age. In 1852, his father arranged to have one of Howells' poems published in the Ohio State Journal without telling him.

He wrote his first novel, The Wedding Journey, in 1872, but his literary reputation took off with the realist novel, A Modern Instance, published in 1882, which described the decay of a marriage. His 1885 novel The Rise of Silas Lapham is perhaps his best known, describing the rise and fall of an American entrepreneur in the paint business. His social views were also strongly reflected in the novels Annie Kilburn (1888) and A Hazard of New Fortunes (1890). He was particularly outraged by the trials resulting from the Haymarket Riot.

In 1904, he was one of the first seven chosen for membership in the American Academy of Arts and Letters, of which he became president.

Choose from Thousands of 1stWorldLibrary Classics By

A. M. Barnard	Booth Tarkington	Edward Everett Hale
Ada Leverson	Boyd Cable	Edward J. O'Biren
Adolphus William Ward	Bram Stoker	Edward S. Ellis
Aesop	C. Collodi	Edwin L. Arnold
Agatha Christie	C. E. Orr	Eleanor Atkins
Alexander Aaronsohn	C. M. Ingleby	Eleanor Hallowell Abbott
Alexander Kielland	Carolyn Wells	Eliot Gregory
Alexandre Dumas	Catherine Parr Traill	Elizabeth Gaskell
Alfred Gatty	Charles A. Eastman	Elizabeth McCracken
Alfred Ollivant	Charles Amory Beach	Elizabeth Von Arnim
Alice Duer Miller	Charles Dickens	Ellem Key
Alice Turner Curtis	Charles Dudley Warner	Emerson Hough
Alice Dunbar	Charles Farrar Browne	Emilie F. Carlen
Allen Chapman	Charles Ives	Emily Bronte
Alleyne Ireland	Charles Kingsley	Emily Dickinson
Ambrose Bierce	Charles Klein	Enid Bagnold
Amelia E. Barr	Charles Hanson Towne	Enilor Macartney Lane
Amory H. Bradford	Charles Lathrop Pack	Erasmus W. Jones
Andrew Lang	Charles Romyn Dake	Ernie Howard Pie
Andrew McFarland Davis	Charles Whibley	Ethel May Dell
Andy Adams	Charles Willing Beale	Ethel Turner
Angela Brazil	Charlotte M. Braeme	Ethel Watts Mumford
Anna Alice Chapin	Charlotte M. Yonge	Eugene Sue
Anna Sewell	Charlotte Perkins Stetson	Eugenie Foa
Annie Besant	Clair W. Hayes	Eugene Wood
Annie Hamilton Donnell	Clarence Day Jr.	Eustace Hale Ball
Annie Payson Call	Clarence E. Mulford	Evelyn Everett-green
Annie Roe Carr	Clemence Housman	Everard Cotes
Annonaymous	Confucius	F. H. Cheley
Anton Chekhov	Coningsby Dawson	F. J. Cross
Archibald Lee Fletcher	Cornelis DeWitt Wilcox	F. Marion Crawford
Arnold Bennett	Cyril Burleigh	Fannie E. Newberry
Arthur C. Benson	D. H. Lawrence	Federick Austin Ogg
Arthur Conan Doyle	Daniel Defoe	Ferdinand Ossendowski
Arthur M. Winfield	David Garnett	Fergus Hume
Arthur Ransome	Dinah Craik	Florence A. Kilpatrick
Arthur Schnitzler	Don Carlos Janes	Fremont B. Deering
Arthur Train	Donald Keyhoe	Francis Bacon
Atticus	Dorothy Kilner	Francis Darwin
B.H. Baden-Powell	Dougan Clark	Frances Hodgson Burnett
B. M. Bower	Douglas Fairbanks	Frances Parkinson Keyes
B. C. Chatterjee	E. Nesbit	Frank Gee Patchin
Baroness Emmuska Orczy	E. P. Roe	Frank Harris
Baroness Orczy	E. Phillips Oppenheim	Frank Jewett Mather
Basil King	E. S. Brooks	Frank L. Packard
Bayard Taylor	Earl Barnes	Frank V. Webster
Ben Macomber	Edgar Rice Burroughs	Frederic Stewart Isham
Bertha Muzzy Bower	Edith Van Dyne	Frederick Trevor Hill
Bjornstjerne Bjornson	Edith Wharton	Frederick Winslow Taylor

Friedrich Kerst
Friedrich Nietzsche
Fyodor Dostoyevsky
G.A. Henty
G.K. Chesterton
Gabrielle E. Jackson
Garrett P. Serviss
Gaston Leroux
George A. Warren
George Ade
Geroge Bernard Shaw
George Cary Eggleston
George Durston
George Ebers
George Eliot
George Gissing
George MacDonald
George Meredith
George Orwell
George Sylvester Viereck
George Tucker
George W. Cable
George Wharton James
Gertrude Atherton
Gordon Casserly
Grace E. King
Grace Gallatin
Grace Greenwood
Grant Allen
Guillermo A. Sherwell
Gulielma Zollinger
Gustav Flaubert
H. A. Cody
H. B. Irving
H.C. Bailey
H. G. Wells
H. H. Munro
H. Irving Hancock
H. R. Naylor
H. Rider Haggard
H. W. C. Davis
Haldeman Julius
Hall Caine
Hamilton Wright Mabie
Hans Christian Andersen
Harold Avery
Harold McGrath
Harriet Beecher Stowe
Harry Castlemon
Harry Coghill
Harry Houidini

Hayden Carruth
Helent Hunt Jackson
Helen Nicolay
Hendrik Conscience
Hendy David Thoreau
Henri Barbusse
Henrik Ibsen
Henry Adams
Henry Ford
Henry Frost
Henry James
Henry Jones Ford
Henry Seton Merriman
Henry W Longfellow
Herbert A. Giles
Herbert Carter
Herbert N. Casson
Herman Hesse
Hildegard G. Frey
Homer
Honore De Balzac
Horace B. Day
Horace Walpole
Horatio Alger Jr.
Howard Pyle
Howard R. Garis
Hugh Lofting
Hugh Walpole
Humphry Ward
Ian Maclaren
Inez Haynes Gillmore
Irving Bacheller
Isabel Cecilia Williams
Isabel Hornibrook
Israel Abrahams
Ivan Turgenev
J.G.Austin
J. Henri Fabre
J. M. Barrie
J. M. Walsh
J. Macdonald Oxley
J. R. Miller
J. S. Fletcher
J. S. Knowles
J. Storer Clouston
J. W. Duffield
Jack London
Jacob Abbott
James Allen
James Andrews
James Baldwin

James Branch Cabell
James DeMille
James Joyce
James Lane Allen
James Lane Allen
James Oliver Curwood
James Oppenheim
James Otis
James R. Driscoll
Jane Abbott
Jane Austen
Jane L. Stewart
Janet Aldridge
Jens Peter Jacobsen
Jerome K. Jerome
Jessie Graham Flower
John Buchan
John Burroughs
John Cournos
John F. Kennedy
John Gay
John Glasworthy
John Habberton
John Joy Bell
John Kendrick Bangs
John Milton
John Philip Sousa
John Taintor Foote
Jonas Lauritz Idemil Lie
Jonathan Swift
Joseph A. Altsheler
Joseph Carey
Joseph Conrad
Joseph E. Badger Jr
Joseph Hergesheimer
Joseph Jacobs
Jules Vernes
Julian Hawthrone
Julie A Lippmann
Justin Huntly McCarthy
Kakuzo Okakura
Karle Wilson Baker
Kate Chopin
Kenneth Grahame
Kenneth McGaffey
Kate Langley Bosher
Kate Langley Bosher
Katherine Cecil Thurston
Katherine Stokes
L. A. Abbot
L. T. Meade

L. Frank Baum
Latta Griswold
Laura Dent Crane
Laura Lee Hope
Laurence Housman
Lawrence Beasley
Leo Tolstoy
Leonid Andreyev
Lewis Carroll
Lewis Sperry Chafer
Lilian Bell
Lloyd Osbourne
Louis Hughes
Louis Joseph Vance
Louis Tracy
Louisa May Alcott
Lucy Fitch Perkins
Lucy Maud Montgomery
Luther Benson
Lydia Miller Middleton
Lyndon Orr
M. Corvus
M. H. Adams
Margaret E. Sangster
Margret Howth
Margaret Vandercook
Margaret W. Hungerford
Margret Penrose
Maria Edgeworth
Maria Thompson Daviess
Mariano Azuela
Marion Polk Angellotti
Mark Overton
Mark Twain
Mary Austin
Mary Catherine Crowley
Mary Cole
Mary Hastings Bradley
Mary Roberts Rinehart
Mary Rowlandson
M. Wollstonecraft Shelley
Maud Lindsay
Max Beerbohm
Myra Kelly
Nathaniel Hawthrone
Nicolo Machiavelli
O. F. Walton
Oscar Wilde
Owen Johnson
P.G. Wodehouse
Paul and Mabel Thorne

Paul G. Tomlinson
Paul Severing
Percy Brebner
Percy Keese Fitzhugh
Peter B. Kyne
Plato
Quincy Allen
R. Derby Holmes
R. L. Stevenson
R. S. Ball
Rabindranath Tagore
Rahul Alvares
Ralph Bonehill
Ralph Henry Barbour
Ralph Victor
Ralph Waldo Emmerson
Rene Descartes
Ray Cummings
Rex Beach
Rex E. Beach
Richard Harding Davis
Richard Jefferies
Richard Le Gallienne
Robert Barr
Robert Frost
Robert Gordon Anderson
Robert L. Drake
Robert Lansing
Robert Lynd
Robert Michael Ballantyne
Robert W. Chambers
Rosa Nouchette Carey
Rudyard Kipling
Saint Augustine
Samuel B. Allison
Samuel Hopkins Adams
Sarah Bernhardt
Sarah C. Hallowell
Selma Lagerlof
Sherwood Anderson
Sigmund Freud
Standish O'Grady
Stanley Weyman
Stella Benson
Stella M. Francis
Stephen Crane
Stewart Edward White
Stijn Streuvels
Swami Abhedananda
Swami Parmananda
T. S. Ackland

T. S. Arthur
The Princess Der Ling
Thomas A. Janvier
Thomas A Kempis
Thomas Anderton
Thomas Bailey Aldrich
Thomas Bulfinch
Thomas De Quincey
Thomas Dixon
Thomas H. Huxley
Thomas Hardy
Thomas More
Thornton W. Burgess
U. S. Grant
Upton Sinclair
Valentine Williams
Various Authors
Vaughan Kester
Victor Appleton
Victor G. Durham
Victoria Cross
Virginia Woolf
Wadsworth Camp
Walter Camp
Walter Scott
Washington Irving
Wilbur Lawton
Wilkie Collins
Willa Cather
Willard F. Baker
William Dean Howells
William le Queux
W. Makepeace Thackeray
William W. Walter
William Shakespeare
Winston Churchill
Yei Theodora Ozaki
Yogi Ramacharaka
Young E. Allison
Zane Grey